Chris Harrison was born in September 1952, the fourth of five children and the only girl. From the age of seven, she wanted to be a nurse, and fulfilled this in 1972 when she passed her finals. Chris married Ian in 1973 and lived in a mobile home until moving into rented accommodation where Jenny joined the family.

Chris hurt her back nursing and finally ended up in a wheelchair. She kept herself busy with toy-making, making over eighty types of soft fur toys, making her own clothes and teaching herself cake decorating and of course, doing all the household chores too. Chris is a busy type of person and is always on the go and likes nothing more than a new challenge. From recovering furniture, making curtains, etc. and now learning to draw and paint. This artistic streak goes out into the garden as she fills her sixty or more tubs with flowers.

Jenny helped Chris to get through all the difficult times by sitting and listening to her innermost thoughts through the long sleepless nights when pain would override sleep and by being her constant companion throughout the days.

Chris and Ian are Christians and are members of the local Methodist Church in Duston, Northampton. They now have a Yorkshire terrier called Tammy – but that's another story!

JENNY, HER OWN STORY

Chris Harrison

JENNY, HER OWN STORY

Chris Harrison

ATHENA PRESS
LONDON

JENNY, HER OWN STORY
Copyright © Chris Harrison 2004

All Rights Reserved

No part of this book may be reproduced in any form
by photocopying or by any electronic or mechanical means,
including information storage or retrieval systems,
without permission in writing from both the copyright
owner and the publisher of this book.

ISBN 1 84401 366 9

First Published 2004
ATHENA PRESS
Queen's House, 2 Holly Road
Twickenham TW1 4EG
United Kingdom

Printed for Athena Press

With grateful thanks to Mrs Marianne Waite.

CHAPTER ONE

MY EARLIEST MEMORY IS OF WHAT, AT THE TIME, seemed to be a very large hut in a garden, which I later found out to be called a kennel. I was there with my two sisters. We were only ten weeks old and so small I could easily fit in the dish that was put out for our water. I know this because I accidentally fell over and landed in it one day.

I cannot now remember why we were there or why our mother wasn't with us. In fact, I cannot remember anything about our mother at all. The people who were looking after us were kind and tended to our every need, but we felt that we would not be staying at this place for long. It was a happy time. We didn't have a care in the world; we just spent our time playing together.

One day, we were out in the sunshine playing as usual. My sisters were playing chase while I sat and watched. I overheard the lady and man talking as they put our food out for us, and what they were saying worried me. The lady said that a man was coming that afternoon to have a look at the black and tan puppies with a view to having one of them. I knew she was talking about us because we were the only black and tan puppies there. I hoped this man would not come because I instinctively knew that if he did, one of us would not be sleeping in our cosy kennel that night. I did not share my thoughts with my sisters, I just let them play and enjoy the rest of the day. They played together a lot. I was more of a loner, but we were a close little trio really.

It was now late afternoon going on into evening. I began to think this man wasn't going to turn up. I was pleased and started to relax a little. After a while I heard the sound of voices coming towards us. I recognised the lady's voice, but I didn't recognise the voice of the man at all. I started to get worried; was this the man who would split up my little family forever? My sisters continued to play, but I just sat and watched the man's every move. The man seemed quite nice. He bent down and called out to me. He put his hand out as if to encourage me to go up to him. I didn't feel frightened. He fussed me for a while and I returned his affection. We seemed to get on well straight away. The man said he had a lady at home called Chris, who would give me a lot of love and really take care of me. He asked if I would like to go home with him. I knew we were there to be taken by people to their homes and live as part of their family. This man did seem nice, and although I hadn't met this lady he was on about, I trusted his judgement.

My heart was torn between staying with my sisters and going with this man whom I knew nothing about, but within a few days my sisters would also have families of their own to go to. I had to go wherever I was sent, though; I didn't really have any choice, did I? I said a fond farewell to my sisters and hoped they would be all right. I felt really sad at the thought I would never see them again...

My sisters watched as I was taken away. I looked around the man's arm so I could see my sisters, and tears came to my eyes as they disappeared from my sight...

The man picked me up and eventually put me on a seat by the side of him. We seemed to be in a sort of big box that had light coming in on several sides. It was warm and comfortable. A door was shut and then we were encased on all sides. I didn't feel too worried to start with, but then I felt a sort of movement. We weren't moving – but this box thing we were sitting in certainly was, because I could see the sky and trees go passing by us. I now began to get worried and felt really frightened. The box stopped but the sound it was making continued. I thought it was all over but then we moved off again! I couldn't cope with it any more – I wanted to run away and be back with my sisters, but I knew that was impossible. Despite my fear at its height, I took my life in my paws. Slowly and carefully I clambered from my soft seat over to the man's lap; it was very difficult. I sat between his legs so he could comfort me. He patted my head as if to say I could stay there. I felt my fear gradually disappear, and with the sound and rocking motion of the box I eventually fell into a deep sleep... I was so tired after the adventures of the day I dreamed of the place I was going to. I wondered what the lady looked like, and would she give me all that love like the man said. Would she be as nice as I hoped...?

CHAPTER TWO

I WAS WOKEN BY THE JOLT OF THE BOX STOPPING. For a second or two I didn't know where I was. I had expected to still be with my sisters – that is, until the man spoke to me and brought me back to reality. Then I remembered I was on my way to my new home. I was very nervous, but at the same time excited. After all, it was going to be a new beginning. The man picked me up and carried me to a house. There were lots of houses all in a row, unlike the place I had just left which stood on its own. I did wonder how these people remembered which house was theirs because they all looked the same to me. As the man unlocked the door he put me in the palm of his other hand and I fitted snugly. He told me not to be frightened as everything would be all right.

Once inside the house I could hear two voices; one was a man's voice and the other was a lady's. I was carried down a dark passageway into a room at the end where the voices were coming from. I was now getting nervous again; my heart was beating so fast I thought it would burst. Was this where I would be living? The lady asked why the man was late, then she saw there was something in his hand. The lady looked down at me and smiled, so I put my tongue out as if to kiss her. She seemed to like me. She took hold of me and held me close to her cheek and said, "Oh, you lovely little thing. You're so sweet!" Then she kissed me.

I didn't understand what she was saying, but it must have been good because she was smiling at me. Her voice sounded kind and she gave me a lot of fuss. I knew then I would be well looked after and loved. The other man that was in the room gave me the name of Jenny. He named me because the lady didn't know what to call me, but she seemed to like the name Jenny. She thought it suited me really well, and I thought it did too. That was my first meeting with my new family ever. It was just going to be the two of them, because the man who named me left after a short while. I felt pleased at how things had gone. My fears all went away after seeing the reaction of the lady.

Introductions over, I was now feeling hungry. I wondered when I would be fed and what the food was going to be like. "I bet you are hungry," the lady said as she carried me into another room. She opened a door and got some milk out and put it into a container. We then moved over to a thing that lit up and got warm, where the lady put the container of milk. An oval-shaped biscuit thing was put into a dish and a yellow round thing with a see-through jelly around it was also put in the dish. The milk was added and it was all mixed up to make a smooth paste to make it easy for me to eat. As the lady made this for me, she told me she had never looked after a puppy or even a dog before. She didn't even know I was coming to live with her, so she didn't have any 'proper' dog food to give me. She said she would do her best, but as it was all new to her, so it would be trial and error, with a lot of love thrown in for good measure. I would have to bear with her. I didn't know she had a bear as well. I hadn't heard or seen it, and they are very big, so I am told! I enjoyed my meal, and thought, It's new to me, so we will have to learn together... Still not too sure of the bear, though.

I liked this lady. I felt safe when she was in sight. While I ate my meal the lady went out of the room. As she left she said she would find something to make me a bed so it would be ready for me when I had finished eating. She wasn't back by the time I had eaten, and all of a sudden I realised I was alone. That room suddenly became very big and the walls seemed to be tall. I felt alone and cried. I was frightened and called out to her. I thought as long as she was in sight again I would be all right. The lady came back again carrying a box with a blanket in it. "What's all this noise for? Did you think I was going to leave you on your own all night?" She picked me up and gave me some fuss to calm me down again, so I gave her a kiss to show I appreciated it.

Time was getting on and I was tired. I think the lady was tired too. They both had a drink and I was given a drop of milky water. After a short time the lady said she was taking me upstairs to bed. My box was put at the side of the bed where the lady was going to sleep. I liked that because I wanted her to be near to me. I felt safer if I could see her. After all, it was my first night in a new home with people I didn't know, and I didn't have my sisters around to give me comfort, did I?

The lady and man got into their beds, then, all of a sudden, it went very dark! Well, I couldn't see the lady any more so I cried.

The lady spoke to me, then I felt her hand just

touch the top of my head. I was comforted by this a little, but I still cried. All I could think of was my sisters lying in the kennel, all cosy together, while I was in my bed alone. After what seemed ages the lady put the light on, got out of bed, and left the room. This made me panic even more. I began to shake. Don't leave me, please don't leave me, I thought as the lady disappeared. A few moments later she came back and put something on the bottom of the bed on her side. The man slept all the while the lady was doing this. I don't know why. Didn't he understand I was upset? The lady then picked me up and quietly said, "Don't worry, Mummy's here. I wouldn't let anything hurt you. I know, you are missing your sisters and you're only tiny." How did she know that? I didn't tell her! She put me on top of her bed on a towel or something. I licked her cheek, then she got back into bed and put the light out.

Now is my chance to get close to this lady, I thought. I made my way up to the top of the bed. It was hard work climbing over all the hills and dips. I was very tired too, but I was determined and I managed it. When I reached the top I could see the lady's head. Nearly there now, then I shall be with her. The covers were slightly open so I quickly went under them. I hoped the lady would let me stay with her and not put me back at the bottom of the bed. I turned around in a circle a couple of times and then lay down with my nose under the lady's chin. I gave out a big sigh; I felt comfortable, warm and safe. Now at last I could go to sleep. The lady took the towel from the bottom of the bed and pushed it under me. I gave a contented grunt as the lady got back into bed. I got myself back into position, then I kissed her on the chin. I felt her hand on my head and she kissed me saying, "Mummy's here, Mummy's here. You go to sleep now, you are safe with me."

That's another time she called herself Mummy. I like that. Yes, I will call her Mummy all the time now. I am going to be all right living with this lady. She is as nice as the man said she would be.

With that thought, I fell fast asleep...

CHAPTER THREE

I WAS WOKEN THE FOLLOWING MORNING BY MY mum stroking me and softly saying, "Come on baby, it's time to get up. I've got some work to do and you have to look around your new home and explore the garden."

After Mum had lifted me out of the bed she said, "You are a good girl. You haven't wet the towel. I will have to get you down the stairs quickly so you can spend a penny."

I didn't understand what she meant really, but I went along with her anyway. We got to a door and Mum said, "Go and do a wee-wee for Mummy there's a good girl, do a wee-wee." Well, I had heard that word before, so I now knew what she was on about. I trotted down the path, onto some grass and did my wee-wee. To be honest I really needed to do one by now. My Mum was so pleased with me she said, "Who's a clever girl then – you are a good girl." I don't know why she thought I was a clever girl. After all, I only did what comes naturally, didn't I? She gave me a kiss on the nose and said, "It's time for your breakfast now, and after that you can go and explore a little."

I don't know where the man was who went to bed the night before; I hadn't seen him so far this morning. I had a nice day. My mum played with me, gave me cuddles, and I had lots of drinks of milky water with a light meal halfway through the day. My day was so filled with different sights, smells and sounds I didn't even have time to miss my sisters.

When evening came the man came home. Mum said, "That's your Daddy. He has come home from work. In a couple of days' time you will go to work with him because I have to go to my work. You won't be left at home on your own. Let's go and see your dad then, go and say hello, tell him you are pleased to see him."

I know that I can call the man, "Dad". It's a lot nicer than calling him the man, don't you think?

After a while we had what they call "dinner". My dinner was different from the other meals I'd had. This meal came out of a thing called a tin and it was specially made for puppies my age. My Mum showed me the tin and said, "This looks nice. Look, it's all for you. If you eat it all up you can have one of these biscuits your Dad bought you from the shop."

I didn't know what a shop was, but it all sounded very nice, didn't it? So I had all my dinner, then was given my biscuit afterwards and I enjoyed all of it.

It was now time for bed again. Before going up the stairs I was taken out into the garden to do my wee-wee, so hopefully I would not wet too much through the night. I got the now expected praise as I performed. On the way up the stairs I wondered where I would sleep tonight. Would I be expected to sleep in my bed on the floor, or would I sleep with my mum all cosy and safe with my nose next to her chin again? I could only hope for the latter, couldn't I?

In the bedroom I was unfortunately put into my bed and eventually Mum and Dad got into theirs.

Then it all went very dark again. I didn't like it so I called out to Mum, but she told me to go to bye-byes (I think that meant sleep). I wanted to go to bye-byes with my mum, so I cried until she gave in and put me in bed with her again on the towel. I knew if I cried long enough she would; she's like that. As soon as I was tucked up in Mum's bed with my nose in the usual position I fell fast asleep.

The following day both Mum and Dad were at home. They had a day off work. They said they were going to take me to see the lady who owned the house; this lady was now living where Mum worked. We went in the box that moved (I have now been told that it is called a car). We stopped at a place that had a big house with lots of little houses around it in its large grounds. We went through two sets of doors and down a corridor into a room. The lady was old. She didn't seem too happy to see me. This puzzled Mum and Dad because the lady had had a dog herself before moving in to this home. I heard her tell my mum either they get rid of me or they will have to move out of her house.

This worried me, as you can imagine, because I liked my mum and dad. I thought I would have to be sent away. I couldn't bear that because I really loved my mum. If I was sent away I might not have such a nice Mum next time. I started to panic. Mum tried to talk to the lady and convince her I wouldn't damage her house in any way, but she wouldn't change her mind at all. I tried to change her mind too by kissing her and being very friendly, but it didn't work. She didn't even want me to sit on her lap!

Back home, Mum and Dad shouted at each other. I

suppose this was because they were worried. Seeing them like that really upset me. I crouched down behind Mum's legs – I felt it was all my fault. I wish we had never gone to see that lady, then she wouldn't have known I was living there. It was now lunchtime. Mum didn't eat much at all; she was crying too. Because Mum was so upset I couldn't eat either. Dad still had his dinner, though. The fact is, I was going to make Mum and Dad lose their home if they kept me, so it's obvious they will have to send me away. They can't keep me, can they?

For the rest of the day I stayed close to my mum. She knew I was upset. She tried to stop me worrying by telling me everything would be all right, but I could tell by her voice that she was very concerned about it all.

The following day Mum had to go into work so I went to work with my dad for the first time. I was taken up some stairs into quite a large room. There were several men there and they all gave me some fuss. Being here for the day would hopefully take my mind off my worries. I had a nice day really. I had my lunch with Dad and some of the men gave me little bits and pieces from their boxes. By the end of the afternoon I was tired and ready to go home.

Although I had been with my dad I missed Mum. I had been left on my own a lot, which never happened when I stayed at home with my mum. At home I ran straight up to my mum, squeaking with delight and wagging my tail so much I thought it would drop off. I kissed Mum all over her face when she picked me up. Mum hugged and kissed me. She told me how much she had missed me. Mum asked me if I had enjoyed my day and I told her what I had been doing. Mum then said, "I have good news for you both." We waited to hear what Mum had to say. "I think I have found us somewhere to live. It's only over the road and down the street a little. The only thing is, I don't know what it will be like. We must go and see it in half an hour's time."

Wow! This is the best news I could have had. Maybe I won't have to be sent away after all!

We went down the road – Mum carried me; it really wasn't far to go at all. An elderly lady opened the door and showed us around what she called "the flat". We would have to share a front door. The rooms were big and they looked very dirty too. Mum and Dad talked for a while, then they said they would take it. (I wasn't too sure where they would take it; there wasn't room for it where we lived now!) Mum said something about it only being for a few months until the house where they were going to live was ready. That was the first time I had heard about another house; how many were we going to have, I wondered! I had thought that the place we were living now would be where I would live forever. Just as well, really, because I didn't like it. It was so old and dark and to be honest it made me feel uneasy. I am not quite sure why. Now I could be happy. I was going to stay with Mum and Dad and not be sent away to another family to start again. You can't imagine how happy I felt. Mum and Dad looked much happier too. We all felt a big weight had been lifted from us.

Back home Mum and Dad had what they called a "chip-shop dinner" because time was getting on.

Mum said she didn't feel like getting a meal ready, so I had a little bit of Mum's white stuff, called fish. I wasn't too sure to start with, so I took a little nibble of it just to try. It was very nice so I ate the rest of it. Mum said it was a celebration meal because I could stay with them. Although I had only known my family a couple of days, I knew Mum wouldn't have let me go away without trying very hard to keep me. She loved me too much to let that happen.

I was so happy I ran around in circles getting nowhere, kissing Mum each time I passed by her legs. Mum laughed, picked me up and started to hug and kiss me. My Dad just laughed. The flat place wasn't very nice really. I think Mum and Dad only said they would have it so they could keep me. As Mum said, we would only be there for a short while until our real house was built. I wonder what that will be like – I can't wait to see it.

The following day Mum and Dad had to get some shopping (that's things to eat and anything else they might need). I couldn't go because dogs are not allowed in shop places, so I would be left on my own until they got back. I was shut in the long dark hallway. The light was left on, but it was still quite dark. I didn't like it so I cried as they were leaving, but Mum said they wouldn't be gone long. After crying for a while I decided to explore this hallway in greater detail. It would help to pass the time until they came back. I walked up to each door in turn and had a look and a bit of a sniff at it – nothing of any interest there really. Now I sat at the bottom of the stairs looking up towards the top. Could I? I have been up them when Mum has carried me and they didn't seem too difficult to climb: well, Mum and Dad did it easily enough. I got my front paws on the first stair; it was bigger than it looked from Mum's arms. I had to really push hard with my back legs while pulling with my front legs. I even tried giving little jumps with my back legs to help. Eventually I managed to get one back paw on the stair and then I gave an extra push and my other paw came up too. Now I had worked out how to get myself on the bottom stair I could start climbing the rest. It would be easy now, wouldn't it?

I got myself about halfway up the stairs; I was exhausted. I looked up and saw the long climb that stood before me, then I looked down at the stairs I had already climbed. It made me feel dizzy, I began to wish I hadn't started to climb them in the first place. Now I was halfway. I didn't know whether I should carry on and struggle to the top, or should I work out a way of getting back down? I tried, but as I couldn't work out a way of getting back down again I only had one choice. I had to struggle to the top. It must have taken me ages and I felt weak, wobbly and tired by the time I reached the top, so I lay down to have a rest.

I must have fallen asleep, because I was woken up by the sound of Mum and Dad calling me. Mum's voice sounded worried. I don't know why. Then she called out, "Jenny, where are you?" Well, I wondered what all the noise was about, so I went to the top of the stairs and whimpered a little so Mum could see where I was. When Mum heard me she came to the bottom of the stairs, looked up and screamed, "Jenny!" I couldn't understand what all the fuss was about. I gave out a little bark and wagged my tail. Mum ran up the stairs and said, "Oh, Jenny, I couldn't find you. I thought you were lost somehow. You shouldn't climb the stairs on your own. You might fall and hurt yourself." With that, Mum thankfully picked me up and carried me downstairs again. Believe me, I won't ever do that on my own again – well, not until I am bigger anyway.

I was hungry now, so Mum made a drink and we all had a thing called a biscuit. My biscuit was dipped into Mum's cup of tea to make it softer. It was very nice. I was glad to get to bed after such an exciting day. I was totally exhausted. By the way, Mum put me straight into bed with her this time. I don't think I will ever use my bed, do you?

For the rest of the week, in the evenings, Mum and Dad packed things into little boxes. Mum said we would be moving into the other place at the weekend. I didn't really know when that would be, but it couldn't be too many days away because Mum packed a lot of clothes and things she normally used. It was a busy time because both Mum and Dad worked during these days. I, of course, went to work with my dad, but after dinner I went with Mum to help her with the packing. I was quite excited really. It would be my second move in a few days. I was glad to get out of that old house, though, but this new place didn't look any better. As Mum said, it was only for a few short months and then we would move again to our house that was still being built. It all sounds very good. I must try and find out more about it. You never know, it may have a big piece of grass for me to play on like I had with my sisters.

The weekend came. We were all up early, then the man that named me came. He was going to help us move all our things to the new home across the road. By lunchtime everything had been moved. We didn't have much of what they called "furniture", and no carpets at all so it didn't take long. While Mum and Dad sorted things out I went to explore. Mum said I could only explore in the room she was in because the hallway went to some stairs that led to the old lady's place and I wasn't allowed there. I didn't like this place. I don't think Mum liked it either, because she cried a little when she thought I wasn't looking. I had to make things better for my mum. I ran up to her, wagging my tail and squeaking, until she picked me up, and then I kissed her. Mum smiled and said, "It's all right. I'll be all right when I've got it clean and it's not for too long. At least I've still got you and that's all that matters to me." Then she hugged and kissed me, so I helped her to sort out the rest of the boxes. I didn't like to see my mum cry. I realised then that Mum needed me just as much as I needed her. I would look after her like she looked after me from now on.

Bedtime came. Mum didn't take my bed into the bedroom, she just took me straight into her bed. Mum said I could always sleep with her at night and only use my bed when I wanted to during the day. Believe me, I didn't argue with her, I just snuggled up and went to sleep. It had been yet another busy day.

CHAPTER FOUR

NOW WE WERE ALL SORTED OUT IN THE FLAT, Mum said she would start to train me. I didn't know what she meant really. What did I have to be trained in? Whatever it was, I would do it the best I could; after all, I wanted to do all I could to make Mum happy after making them move house.

When Mum had finished her jobs around the flat, she took me into the room where the settees were – I think it's called the "lounge" room. Mum got on the floor with me and said, "Right, Jenny I want you to sit." As Mum said the word "sit", she pushed my bottom down on the floor so I had to bend my legs until my bottom was on the floor. Well, I knew how to sit, but I didn't know that was the word to use when you did it! As my bottom touched the floor, Mum said the word several times over and then said, "Good girl, you are clever." Mum gave me some fuss and a kiss on the nose. We had a little play with my ball then all of a sudden Mum said, "Jenny, sit." Well, I wasn't ready for it, so I didn't sit straight away, so Mum put her hand on my bottom until I sat down. Then I remembered the word. Next time I thought, I will be ready for it. We had a play with the ball again but this time when Mum said, "Sit," I put my bottom down straight away – well, more or less. She was so pleased with me she said, "Clever girl, very good, I am so proud of you. You will have to show your dad how clever you are in a few days' time." Mum picked me up, and hugged and kissed me while still praising me. I, in return, squeaked with delight and wagged my tail with excitement. Yes, I thought I was clever too!

All through the rest of the day Mum would suddenly say, "Sit!" Sometimes I remembered the word and other times – well, you know, when I was busy, I would forget. The times I forgot to do it Mum would say the word again while pushing my bottom to the floor. She would repeat the word over and over again to make me remember it. The times I did it on what Mum calls "first command", I would get full praise. I enjoyed it really. It was a bit like a game, so I would enjoy my training and learn quicker. I thought that if all my training is as easy as this I should soon finish it.

Through the rest of the week all of a sudden, when I would least expect it, Mum would turn to me and say, "Sit!" By the end of the week I was an expert! On the Saturday after Mum came home from work, she told Dad I had something to show him. I felt excited; now was my chance to show off a little. I went running up to Dad, skidding on the floor as I ran. Mum said the words, "Jenny, sit." I remembered the word and sat straight away. Dad was pleased with me and called me a clever girl. He smiled as if to say, that's my girl. Well, that's what I thought he might say. At least I didn't let my mum down, did I?

I was now reaching the grand age of twelve weeks. While having our dinner one day I heard Mum and Dad talking. They were on about taking me to see a "vet" to have something called an injection. I didn't understand what they meant, but if I was going somewhere, to get something, I didn't mind – well, would you? Mum said she would make a thing called an appointment.

The day arrived for my appointment. I was put into the car thing and off we went to the vet. I was getting used to the car now and enjoyed going in it. I felt quite relaxed as I sat on Mum's lap looking out of the window. It was only a short car ride. When the car stopped I was carried into a big house. We went into a room off a small hallway. I saw lots of other animals with their Mums or Dads. There were small and very large dogs and things called cats were in basket-type things with a mesh on one side so they could look out. Other people sat with boxes of all sizes on their laps containing all sorts of animals that I hadn't even heard of, but Mum told me what they were. There was also a very distinctive smell!

All of a sudden it dawned on me that I had been in a place like this before when I lived with my sisters, a few days before I went to live with Mum and Dad. I didn't know these places were called vet's, so the thing they did to me must also have been called an injection. I remembered what that was, and I didn't like it at all. Now I was going to have it done to me again!

A lady called Mum's name and I was carried into another room. As we went into the room I saw a man standing by a thing called a table. It didn't look like our table at home, though. I started to get frightened so I started to shake and cry. I tried to cling to my mum as she put me on the table. I was so frightened, I'm afraid I disgraced myself and made a large puddle right in the middle of the man's clean table. The man smiled and told Mum not to worry as he wiped it all clean again. The next second I felt a small sharp pain in the skin around the back of my neck. I screamed out loud to let them know I didn't like it. Mum picked me up and fussed me. "There, there, it's all over now. Mummy's got you." I was glad when we got out of that place and were back home again. I could smell the dreadful scent of that place in our lounge. I think it was because the vet man rubbed something onto my fur before I felt the sharp pain. Mum made us a cup of tea. She said I had been such a good girl I could have a biscuit. I didn't think I had been good at all because of the puddle I made, but I wasn't going to argue with Mum, was I? By nightime I had forgotten about the thing called an injection. I must have needed it or Mum wouldn't have let them do it to me, would she?

When Mum had her next day off she took me to a "pet shop". Inside the shop there were lots of collars and leads of all shapes and sizes. Mum showed me some of them. The collar I had on now was soft and it had something called elastic on it so it could get bigger. I think that was so it was easier for me to take off when I wanted to. I was now going to have a proper collar so a lead could be attached to it. I would be able to go out for a walk with Mum and Dad then. Mum bought me a collar and lead that fitted my size, but I couldn't use it until I had finished some of my training, so Mum carried me back home again.

We arrived back home and had our cup of tea (I love my milky cup of tea that Mum gives me), and my usual biscuit dipped in Mum's tea. Then, after cup of tea time, Mum put my new collar on me; it felt very different from my other one. My first one was soft and not very wide; my new one was made out of something called leather and was about twice the width of my first one. It felt uncomfortable but Mum said I would soon get used to it and forget all about it. I couldn't pull this one off when I wanted to either, unlike the other one. Once Mum put it on me I was stuck with it. Mind you, I did feel grown-up now, and it looked very smart.

When Dad came home from work I ran up to him and showed him my new collar. He liked it and said I looked "posh" (I didn't really know what that meant, but I think it must have been good). By bedtime I had forgotten I was wearing it. Mum took it off me to give me a rest from it for the night, but she said after that I would have to wear it all of the time. When Mum took it off she let me have a look and sniff of it. Mum showed me a little silver barrel that was on the collar. When it was opened there was a piece of paper inside with my name and where I lived written on it. That was in case I got lost at any time and whoever found me could take me back home. I thought, I'm not going to get lost because I wouldn't go anywhere without Mum or Dad.

My training continued. Mum now used the word "sit" as a regular thing until I always sat as soon as she said the word. Now I was going to be taught how to use the collar and lead.

The next day my collar was put back on me and I was told that later in the day my lead would be attached to the ring on the collar. The idea was, I could drag the lead around on the floor to get used to the feel of it pulling on the collar. Mum would do this on and off through the day for half an hour at a time. I thought it was a good idea really. I had to be careful it didn't catch on anything though. Mum was always at hand if it did. Considering my mum hasn't trained a puppy before, she's doing well with all her ideas, don't you think? By late afternoon I didn't mind the lead being there any more. Mind you, I wasn't too keen when it was put on in the first place. I think it helped me knowing what I needed the collar and lead for. After all, if I didn't wear them I couldn't go out for these walks with Mum and Dad like they told me about, could I? And I was looking forward to them.

Over the next few days after work, and after Mum had finished her cup of tea, she would put my lead on for a short while. Sometimes she would pick up the other end of the lead and hold it loosely so I could get used to the feel of it pulling a little. By the end of the week, Mum would pull on it sometimes so I had to go the way Mum wanted to go (even when I wanted to go the other way). Mum said I was doing so well she would take me for my first proper walk outside on her next day off. I was excited by that. I wondered what it would be like walking on the outside with all those other people and things. I couldn't wait to see and hear all the new sights and sounds that were out, in what Mum called "the big wide world".

Mum continued to walk me around the flat on the lead while we waited for the day off to come. I didn't always go the way I was supposed to go. When I didn't Mum would give a little pull on the lead until I went her way. Mum said I have to do as I am told when I am on the lead. If I do I could get hurt when we were out side.

Mum's day off arrived; Dad had to go to work. As it wasn't too far away Mum said that afternoon we would give Dad a surprise and meet him out of work. That way we could walk there and get a ride back in the car with Dad. Mum didn't tell Dad what we were going to do so we could surprise him.

It was about three in the afternoon when we left for our walk. Dad was due to leave off work at five. Mum said it was better to leave that early so we had plenty of time and needn't hurry, especially as it was my first walk. It was a hot day too. My lead was attached to my collar, Mum locked the door and off we went. The pavement (that's what Mum called it, anyway) was hard and it felt hot to the pads on my paws. I walked proudly, as taught, at Mum's side. People looked so big from my level and everywhere seemed so noisy. We turned the corner. Well, if I thought it was busy and noisy before, it was ten times worse now. I suddenly became frightened – cars were whizzing past me at such a speed and there was also a smelly, cloud-like stuff coming from each one of them. It made me feel sick and want to cough. People were pushing past Mum and all I could see was legs all around me. I began to panic. I stood still. Mum gave a little pull on my lead but I was stuck to the spot – I couldn't move. Mum spoke to me and tried to coax me to carry on, but it was all too much for me. She picked me up and carried me for a while. The busy place was called a main road, I was told, so Mum would carry me until we passed by it. Thank goodness for that!

I felt safe being in Mum's arms again. I wasn't so sure I wanted to go for these walks anymore. It wasn't what I had expected.

A short while later Mum said, "I am going to put you down now, Jenny. It's quieter down this street so you will be all right now." Back down on the pavement I started to get frightened again so I put my bottom down. When Mum pulled on my lead, instead of going with her, I sat fast. I thought if I sat, Mum would eventually give in and pick me up again. Mum said, "Come on, Jenny, it's not busy now so you will be all right, I won't let anything hurt you." I took a couple of steps and put my bottom down again; I really wanted to be carried and not do this walking thing.

Mum tried to coax me to walk again and again, but I just kept putting my bottom onto the pavement after every couple of steps. Mum finally said, "Come on, Jenny. I will carry you for a little while. You are getting a big girl now and are too heavy for me to carry for long. If we don't hurry up we will miss your Dad at work and we will have to walk all the way back again, and you wouldn't want that, would you? Anyway, you will enjoy it after a while, you'll see. Just give it a chance." With that, Mum picked me up and carried me for a while. I now felt ashamed of myself. Mum was right; I was too heavy for her to carry for long. I was a big girl now too, and should act like one. I didn't want to miss Dad and have to walk all the way back home again either.

When Mum puts me down again, I thought, I will walk properly and make Mum proud to have me at her side. After all, Mum taught me on the lead around the house, and she's not going to let anything bad happen to me, is she, because she loves me.

After a short while I was put back down again.

Mum said, "Be a good girl now and we shall be in time to meet Dad. He will be so pleased with you."

Now is my chance, I thought. I trotted along side her like we did inside the flat, and do you know, I suddenly started to enjoy myself! Mum pointed things out to me and told me what they were. Yes, I was going to enjoy walks with Mum.

Eventually we turned into the place where Dad worked. I was hot, tired and very thirsty, but after that little problem was over, I enjoyed it all.

Dad was surprised but pleased to see us. He gave Mum a kiss and gave me a lot of fuss too. A nice dish of cool water was put down for me and Mum got a cold drink too. After a while we thankfully all got into the car and went home. After we had eaten our dinners Mum cuddled me on the settee and said, "Well, Jenny, did you enjoy your first walk? You did very well because it was very hot. I will take you on a shorter walk next time so you don't get so tired."

Mum was right; I was tired, but on the whole I had enjoyed myself and would look forward to my next walk. Now I was ready to get into bed and have a long sleep. I think Mum was ready to go to bed too, don't you?

CHAPTER FIVE

A FEW WEEKS LATER, ONE DAY AFTER BREAKFAST, Mum and Dad were talking about going to see how much of our new house had been built. There had been some trouble with things called "foundations" and "vandalism", that had been done a few weeks earlier. I didn't understand what they were talking about, but whatever it was it meant we would have to stay in this place another month. I knew Mum was upset about that. She never said much, but I could tell. Mum and Dad said that they would go and see how far the foundations had progressed when they next had a day off together, which would be on the following Monday.

The day arrived and we all got into the car. I wasn't sure until then that I would be going with them. Mum said, "Jenny, we are going to see where we are going to live, would you like to come and have a look too?" Well, of course I wanted to go. I was dying to see where we would be living. I didn't have a clue where it was or what it looked like. Mum said it had a big kitchen and an even bigger lounge. There were three bedrooms upstairs, too, Mum said. I would also be allowed to go upstairs in our own house. The thing that pleased me the most was the fact we would have a bigger garden for me to run about in.

We were now on our way. Mum said one day, when the weather was better, we would walk around to see it because it wasn't too far away. It was about half an hour's walk, and part of the way would be through a big park. (That's a place like a very big garden with lots of grass and trees where people can go and walk, run or play things called tennis and bowls.) I would be able to have a good run about, first on the way there and again on the way back. I would look forward to that.

We now arrived at the building site – that's where our house was going to be. Well, I could see houses in different stages of being built. Some at the front of this site where we first went in were finished. After seeing the houses at the front I got very excited. I thought if our house is going to be like that it would be wonderful.

I heard Mum and Dad say that these big houses made the estate look "posh". Mum then said, "Yes, they hide the fact that the smaller houses are further back on the estate." The car stopped. We had to walk to see where our house was because the road wasn't finished. Well! What a big disappointment. All I could see of our house was a big square of concrete stuff. Mum and Dad both seemed pleased. I couldn't understand why because there was hardly anything there to see. Mum picked me up and said, "This is it, Jenny. This is where we are going to live, and at the back is where the garden will be." I gave Mum a kiss because she seemed so happy with this grey lump of nothing. There weren't even any walls or anything, so I couldn't really understand what Mum and Dad were so happy about, but I showed them I was happy too!

On the way home Mum said, "You wait, Jenny. In a few weeks you will see a big difference. It will look more of a house then." Mum was so happy she hugged and kissed me, so I showed some enthusiasm as well because I like to see Mum happy. Dad didn't say much at all – he just drove us back home again. He did say he was hungry and wanted his tea. Mum said it was typical of men not to be interested in things. It was decided we would not go and see it again for a month. By then, there would be a big difference. Mum did her best to make the flat what she calls "homely", but it was difficult with boxes everywhere.

While we waited for the month to pass life carried on much as usual. Dad went to work, taking me with him when Mum had to go to her work. Things suddenly changed a little for Mum with her work hours. She had to work three full days and two nights, so things changed for me too. It felt strange not going to bed with Mum these two nights. I still went in the bed, but Dad didn't cuddle and talk to me like Mum did. Mums always seem better than Dads at that sort of thing, so I am told. Well, come to think of it, I did most things with my mum. I knew how my mum was feeling most of the time, too, and she did with me. It wasn't the same with Dad somehow. Still, it's early days. I've not known Mum and Dad for long, but I am glad I came to live with them, even if we did have to move house. Mind you, with Mum working two nights I did have her with me all day. I only had to go to work with Dad the other three days.

On Mum's days off she continued with my training. I did all sorts of things called obedience lessons. I had to learn to do what I was told when I was told to do it, not a minute before or a minute after. I got frustrated at times, but Mum was always patient with me until I got the idea. It was good fun really.

The four weeks soon passed and we went back to see how the house was coming along. As we got nearer and could see a few of the houses in our row, we could see such a difference. There wasn't just the big slab of concrete any more. There were now four partially finished walls rising up from this concrete base. The only thing that worried me was how small this house was going to be. It looked like it was only going to have one room because it didn't have any walls inside it like the flat we lived in now. Mum and Dad walked across from one side to the other. They seemed unconcerned about it only having the one room. Mum called me so I went over to her. She picked me up. "Jenny," she said, "this is where the lounge is going to be and the kitchen is over here at the back." Mum showed me through a gap where there weren't any bricks. "And this Jenny, is the back door. You will be able to go out through there into the garden and run about to your heart's content."

I thought it might be cold in the winter with that big gap there. Mum gave me a big hug and kiss at this point. I liked that. I wagged my tail and kissed my mum on her nose. Mum carried me back to the car because of all the stuff she called rubble. Mum said she was worried about me getting a nail or splinter of wood in my paws. See how my mum looks after me.

We went to see how the house was coming along every two weeks after that. All through the summer we walked to the park as Mum had promised. I was let off my lead so I could have a good run and chase the ball Mum or Dad would throw for me. I don't know why they kept throwing it if they wanted it back again, but you have to humour them sometimes don't you? I was only allowed this freedom in the park because Mum said I was good at "recall" (that's coming straight back to her as soon as she called me). If I wasn't I wouldn't be able to run free off the lead.

One thing that seemed a little odd to me was the fact that Dad would run around with me but not Mum. I did everything else with Mum, so why not run and play in the park together? Mum would say, "Jenny, go and have a run and play with your Dad." I would go off and run and play with Dad but sometimes I would turn and look at Mum. I could see she would be longing to join in. When she thought I wasn't looking her smile would change and a sad, longing look would come on her face. I don't think Dad knew about it because he just kept playing with the ball. I tried to take the ball to Mum once, after Dad had thrown it, but Dad just said, "No, Jenny, Mum can't run about with you, so bring your ball back to me." I did as I was told. I wish he would tell me why Mum can't run with me, then I could understand and maybe be able to help in some way.

Each time we went to the house more and more work had been done. After a few months we went for our usual look at the house and it looked so different. It had two rooms downstairs, as Mum had told me before, but now we could go upstairs and the framework of the walls to divide the rooms was now all in place. We were all very excited because it was the biggest change since we had started coming to look.

"It won't be long now, Jenny. We will soon be out of that dreadful flat and in our own home at last." Mum gave me a big hug as she showed me out of one of the windows. I liked to see Mum so happy.

Mum was right because within four weeks Mum and Dad had a letter from the people who were building our house. They told us a day we could move into our new home. Mum said it would be "our home" then, and not a house because people make a house into a home. Rather nice really. I don't think Mum calls the place we are living in now home. I don't either because it's not nice enough to call home. Mum said she will be glad to see the back of all those boxes and put out all her little nick-nacks, whatever they may be. Maybe I will find out when we move.

As the day got closer Mum was very busy. She would have a shorter sleep the day after working through the previous night, then get up and sort things into boxes that we wouldn't be using. It only seemed to be Mum doing this. Probably it was the sort of thing only Mums did?

By the end of the week Mum had packed and labelled every box she could find. We were going to move some things on the Thursday after Dad got home from work.

Thursday arrived and off we went to see the finished house. We were going to put the curtains up and put a carpet in the lounge. Mum told me that they could only afford carpet for the one room, but she didn't seem to mind about it. "Oh, Jenny," she said, "we will soon be in our own home with our own bits and pieces around us, and we will never have to move again". She hugged me. I was so pleased Mum would finally have the home she wanted and deserved. Apparently, this would be the fifth move within a year, so they deserved a home of their own, don't you think?

Curtains and carpet all sorted out, Mum took me for a last look around before going back to the flat. she talked about her plans for our new home, the decorating (that's putting paper with patterns on it onto the walls), and the furniture they would buy when they could afford it. "Oh Jenny, it will be wonderful for all of us, and you will be able to play in the garden whenever you want to." Mum said she was what she called, "on cloud nine". I didn't understand what that meant (I didn't know clouds had numbers), but I think it must be a nice cloud.

I don't think any of us slept well that night. Bright and early the following morning Dad started to load up the car while Mum packed the last few things. A man came in his car to help us to move. Dad and the man filled his car too. Mum picked me up and we all got into the cars and left that flat behind us. It was a lot cleaner than it was when we went there, I might add. We arrived at our new home. Dad said, "Right, let's start the unloading."

Mum said, "Before we do that, Ian (that's Dad's name), I want you to carry me over the threshold." Mum giggled, Dad gave a sigh, and me, well, I didn't have a clue as to what they were on about.

Dad said, "Do I have to?"

Mum and the man both said, "Yes, you do," at the same time. Dad unlocked the front door, picked Mum up and carried her through the doorway. I followed behind them. Mum, Dad and the man were all laughing. I went running around jumping and squeaking with delight. Dad said, "I'm glad you're not too heavy or I would have dropped you." Mum said he was cheeky and we all laughed again.

By the middle of the afternoon we were almost sorted out. All the boxes and what little furniture Mum and Dad had had now been put in their proper places. I had thoroughly explored all of the house and garden. The garden was just a big patch of mud with one piece of that concrete stuff just outside the back door. Every time I went out Mum had to wipe all the mud off my paws. "The sooner we get part of the garden turfed the better. Then you can play out without going in the mud," Mum said, with a smile on her face as she again wiped the mud of my paws. I kissed Mum on the nose and followed her into the lounge room, but I did wonder what that thing called turf was.

We were all very tired so we had a sit-down before Mum got the tea ready. We went to bed early, we were that tired. It had been a long day though. Mum said all that packing and unpacking had started her pain off again so she needed to lie flat. I didn't know where Mum's pain was, but it must have been bad. I think she was crying because of it. After being in bed a while Mum kissed me and said, "Home at last, Jenny. It's wonderful, don't you think?" I kissed Mum in answer to her question and cuddled up to her. I was lying in the middle of the bed, facing Mum's back with my head on Mum's pillow. Mum said, "Oh Jenny, that's wonderful. It's helping Mummy's back with your tummy warming and supporting me – it's just what I need. You are clever."

So it was Mum's back that hurt her; possibly that's why she can't run with me. I wish I had known sooner because if I had, I would have laid like that all the time to help with the pain. I would do anything to help Mum or Dad because I love them.

This was our first night in our new home. Yes, it was wonderful; Mum was right. I fell asleep dreaming of playing in that garden, that is, when the garden, as Mum put it, is partly turfed! Goodnight Mum, goodnight Dad, and goodnight new home.

CHAPTER SIX

Ever since I first went to live with Mum and Dad they have taken me to see two people who they called "Granny" and "Grandpa". I know they loved these two people a lot because of the way they talked about them and always greeted them with a kiss and a big hug.

Granny and Grandpa were very old and lived in a small bungalow among a group of other bungalows. They walked very slowly and seemed to be unsteady on their feet. I instinctively knew that I must never jump up on them or get under their feet or they might fall over. I greeted them instead by squeaking with delight and wagging my tail with such a force that I thought it might drop off. They in turn greeted me by getting to the nearest chair and sitting down so they could give me some fuss. I too loved Granny and Grandpa. They were very nice and kind people. I can tell instinctively when I first meet people whether I am going to like them or not, and with these two people it was love at first sight. I think it was the same for them with me too.

Granny and Grandpa never came to see us at the flat because Mum said the steps were too difficult for them. Now we are settled in our new home, Mum said they could come when the warmer weather is here. I would enjoy them coming to have tea with us instead of us always going to their home. I want to show off my garden to them. Mum said it would give her time to get things into some sort of order before they came.

As I mentioned before, Mum and Dad didn't have much of what they call furniture. The lounge had two settees, a carpet, a table that wobbled and a thing called a television. This is a square thing that has pictures and music and people talking coming from it. I don't know how. They must have come from inside of it, though, because there was nothing behind the box. Mum or Dad had to press a thing called a button to make it work though. I thought buttons were things on their clothes, but never mind... We look at it in the evenings when Mum says she needs to lie down and rest her back. I joined Mum on her settee. I lay under her legs because it seemed to help her pain thing. I felt comfortable lying like that and I was with my mum and I liked laying with my mum. Dad lay on the other settee in the evenings. He didn't have any pain like Mum. He did it, he said, to relax after a hard day at work at the hospital place.

Upstairs in Mum and Dad's bedroom there was an old carpet that covered most of the floor; a bed; a thing called an ottoman that Mum had before she met Dad; a thing called a leaning, plastic wardrobe; and a chest of drawers Dad had from his Mum and Dad's house. I didn't realise Mums and Dads had a Mum and Dad too! We had an odd piece of carpet and an old bed in the back bedroom and an even smaller front bedroom with just boxes in. The piece that joined these rooms together was called the landing, and that just had several pieces of carpet that didn't match anything or even each other. We didn't have any carpet on the stairs at all. I know we should have done, because that horrible house we were in had it and so did the stairs to that upstairs flat we have just left. None of this mattered to Mum. She was just happy to have a home they could call their own, she told me. Mum kept the house very clean and was happy with what she had. It was good to see her so happy.

The warmer weather came and Granny and Grandpa were brought around to see our new home. By now we had a big armchair that some one gave us and some things called units for Mum to put her nicknacks out instead of leaving them in those boxes. These nick-nacks were things that Mum called ornaments. They were made of hard stuff and made to look like animals and other different shapes. They were of all sizes too. These ornaments don't move or talk; they don't actually do anything at all. Mum just picks them up occasionally and does a thing called dusting, then puts them back down again. I don't understand it really, but Mum likes them so I like them.

I jumped and squealed with delight when Granny and Grandpa arrived, but I kept out of the way so I didn't trip them up as Mum had taught me. Granny went straight to the big chair; Grandpa sat on one of the settees. As soon as Granny sat down I asked Mum to put me on her lap to give her some fuss. Granny kept saying, while pointing a finger at me – which, incidentally, was bent at the end – "Don't you dare lick me, don't you dare." She always said it with a smile on her face and what Mum calls "a twinkle in her eyes", which I took to mean she really wanted me to kiss her so I always duly obliged. "You dirty cat!" she would say. I kept thinking, I'm a dog, not a cat, but Granny is old so I never said anything. After giving Granny some fuss Mum would lift me down so I didn't get caught up in Granny's wire that goes into her ear. I don't know what it's for, though.

I then go and get myself onto the settee and get a lot of fuss from Grandpa. Sometimes I fall asleep on his lap because I get excited and it makes me very tired. Granny and Grandpa stay for tea, then I play with my ball with them. They like that and so do I – it's fun! After a while Dad takes them back to their bungalow but they give me some fuss before they go.

Granny and Grandpa had to leave their bungalow and go into the nursing home because they couldn't look after themselves anymore. They were upset but Mum said they were in their late eighties. I think that must be very old, don't you? I was allowed to go into the nursing home to see them, but it wasn't the same because they only had one room between them. I don't think they were as happy. They didn't seem to be the same as when we went to the bungalow. Dad fetched them several times during the better weather and they always seemed pleased to be in a normal home again. I always did my best to cheer them up when they came. One time Granny came without Grandpa. I looked out of the window to see if he was still in the car but he wasn't. I never saw Grandpa again and Granny seemed lonely and sad. I don't think she saw him again either. No one told me where he was or why he went, but for a while Mum and Dad were upset too. One day Mum said they were going out for the whole morning and she couldn't take me because they were going to Grandpa's funeral. I didn't know where that was, but they didn't seem to be happy about going. I missed Grandpa but I still made a fuss of Granny. In fact, I gave her more fuss because I thought she needed more now.

By the way, I sit in that big chair at the side of Mum in the afternoons, but I always let Granny use it when she comes for tea.

CHAPTER SEVEN

One day Mum told Dad that I should be coming "into season" soon. As I went to the hospital with Dad some days I should be "seen to" so I don't get a lot of dogs coming around me and get pregnant. I didn't understand what getting pregnant was but usually when Mum says I need "seeing too" she means Dad's got to feed me because she is busy. What this pregnant thing has to do with food I wasn't sure. I hadn't heard that word before, but I was sure I would find out eventually what it meant.

Well, it suddenly came to me that Mum fed me a while ago, so why was she asking Dad to feed me again? I waited around near my dish for some time, but Dad never put anything down for me. I got fed up with waiting so I went off and played.

I forgot all about the pregnant thing until the evening when Mum and Dad were talking. Mum said she had phoned the vet and arranged for me to be seen to and have my dew claws done at the same time. I wasn't sure I liked the sound of that, because I had been to the vet before and I didn't like it because he hurt me. I felt sure Mum wouldn't do anything to hurt me though, or come to think of it let any one else hurt me, would she?

It was now Christmas Eve. I had been living with Mum and Dad since the warmer weather started. I think Mum called it spring. I felt I had been living with them a long time – well, all my life really. I couldn't think of being without them now.

Mum didn't give me my breakfast as she usually did; not even a drink, and I was thirsty. Maybe she forgot, although she never forgot before! Mum sat down with me and she looked worried. "Jenny," she said, "Daddy is going to take you to the vet. You will have a sleep and when you wake up your tummy and front paws will be sore. You must not be frightened because Daddy will come and collect you and bring you to the home where Mummy works and Granny lives. You can stay on Granny's bed until we go home."

I didn't understand a word of what she said, but she cried so whatever it was it had upset her. I kissed her to show her I loved her and whatever it was couldn't be that bad, could it? Mum picked me up and hugged me so tight I could hardly breathe. Then she kissed me and said, "Don't worry, I will see you at Granny's, and when we get home I will look after you." I did wonder if this had anything to do with that "pregnant" thing they talked about last week. Well, it certainly didn't have anything to do with food, did it!

I started to get a bit worried now as Dad put me into the car and we drove off. We didn't go the usual way. Then I saw the house where I had that injection thing. Dad took me in and a lady took me away from Dad saying, "She will be all right with us. You can pick her up at four p.m. Don't worry." With that I was taken into another room. I cried. I had never been without Mum or Dad before, I was frightened. I wanted to go to work with my dad! No wonder Mum was upset – she knew I would be on my own without her to keep me calm and safe!

I was put into a cage thing without my own blanket, and left on my own for a while. After what seemed ages the lady came back in, spoke to me and took me out of the cage. I was carried into another room where a man stood. They were both nice and spoke to me. The lady stroked and talked to me while the man started to shave the fur off my paw. I thought Mummy would be cross if she knew what he was doing to me. She was proud of my lovely coat. I didn't like it. I was frightened. Mummy, Mummy, I want my mummy. Where are you, Mummy? I cried. All of a sudden I felt funny and then I fell into a deep sleep.

Very drowsily, I slowly opened my eyes. It was very difficult because my eyelids felt so heavy. I didn't know where I was and as I looked around my head felt heavy and I could see two of everything. I heard the sound of voices in the background but it sounded peculiar; I couldn't understand a word they were saying. I must have gone back to sleep again because the next time I remember anything things seemed a little clearer. I could see better now too. Then all of a sudden, as I tried to move, my tummy felt sore and my front paws felt as if they were being squeezed. Was this what my mummy was trying to tell me this morning, I wondered. A lady came up to my cage thing. She talked to me, stroking my head as she spoke. She sounded kind and it made me feel better and not so afraid. She gave me a little drink of water. It was nice and made my mouth taste better. I still felt sleepy and as she spoke to me I fell back to sleep.

Some time later I was woken by the sound of voices coming towards me. After a few seconds I realised I knew one of them. It was my dad. I remember now; Mummy said I would wake up with a sore tummy and paw, then my dad would come to get me. I was pleased to see my daddy. I gave him a little wag of my tail to show him how pleased I was to see him. I knew I would soon be seeing Mummy now and I would be safe. Dad spoke to the lady; then he carried me out and put me into the car. The fresh air was nice and I felt pleased to get out of that place.

After a short ride in the car, Dad carried me into the nursing home where Mummy worked. The first person I saw was my mummy. I can't tell you how pleased I was. I was so relieved to see her, I whimpered with relief. I knew I would be all right now. Mummy put me onto granny's bed on a towel and covered me with my blanket because I was shivering. Mum gently stroked my head and kissed me. It was good to hear her soft, comforting voice. I felt everything would be all right now I was back with Mum. I went back to sleep, knowing that soon I would be home.

I vaguely remember being in the car and being carried into our house and laid on the settee. I felt cold. Then Mum put something under a blanket and laid me on top of it. It felt warm and soothing. I put my tongue out as if to kiss Mum to show her it comforted me.

After a while I felt I needed to do a wee-wee. I tried to get off the settee but my body felt wobbly and I started to wee-wee just before I got on to the floor. Mum lifted me onto the floor but as I tried to stoop, my bottom refused to stay off the floor. I was upset because I was weeing on Mum's carpet, but Mum smiled at me and lifted my bottom up slightly so I wasn't sitting on my wee-wee. Mum kept saying, "Don't worry baby, it's not your fault, it doesn't matter." When I had finished Mum cleaned me and put me back onto a dry pad that was covering my blanket. Mum gave me a little drink by holding my dish for me so I could drink lying on my warm blanket. I did feel upset as I lay there while Mum cleaned the carpet, but she didn't seem to mind as long as I was all right.

At the end of the evening Dad carried me outside to do my wee-wee while Mum got the bed ready for me with a plastic thing and a towel. I did feel a little better by then, but Dad still had to hold me up a little. I was glad to get into bed and cuddle up to Mum. Mum cuddled me and told me what a good girl I had been. As I lay there I thought to myself, What a day it has been – my first day without either Mum or Dad, in a place I didn't like, having something done to me!

I had slept all night. When I woke up I felt a lot better, apart from needing my breakfast, that is – I was starving. I just felt sore on my tummy and paws but I wasn't wobbly any more. I still didn't really understand what had happened to me the day before. I did have a strange feeling in my front paws. When I got out of bed I noticed my front paws were covered in white stuff. I hadn't really seen it the night before because I felt too tired. Mum made a big fuss of me as I kissed her to wake her up. She looked at my tummy and paws. I don't know what she was looking for.

Maybe she wondered what the white stuff was too. I didn't like this white stuff, so I tried biting it to get it off. Mum gently told me I must leave it alone because it was there to make my paws better. I didn't realise until then that there was anything wrong (apart from the white stuff being there) with my paws. It was obvious to me that if I could take the white stuff off, my paws would feel better as they didn't hurt before it was put there.

There was also something strange about today. After my wee-wee I went into the lounge. Mum and Dad were having breakfast. I noticed that there were lots of things on the floor. All were of different shapes and sizes and covered in brightly coloured paper. After we had finished our breakfast Mum and Dad sat on the floor and started to take the coloured paper off all the things on the floor. Mum showed me each thing as she opened it and told me what it was.

After Mum and Dad had uncovered the things on the floor, Mum picked up one last covered thing that she had put near the thing she called a Christmas tree. "Look, Jenny, this one is for you." Mum unwrapped it for me, while I sat wagging my tail and sniffing at the paper. I could smell chocolate stuff – I like chocolate stuff. When all the paper was off Mum showed me some chocolate buttons and a new ball to play with. I jumped about, wagging my tail and squeaking with delight. I sniffed at my new ball and Mum rolled it across the room so I could get it and take it back to her. (Mums and Dads do that sort of thing; I don't understand why.) As I took the ball back to Mum she said, "Good girl and a Happy Christmas to you". I didn't understand what this "Happy Christmas" was, but if it meant getting new things and chocolate I wasn't going to complain, was I!

Something else about this Happy Christmas – we had a thing called a Christmas Dinner. I had, so Mum told me, turkey, sausage, bacon and vegetables with lots of turkey gravy on it. I didn't care what it was called – I just wanted to eat it all up. After all I didn't get any dinner the day before, did I, so I was very hungry.

After we had had our food and everything was cleared away, I lay on the settee with Mum, and watched the television (the box-thing in the corner of the room), while Dad fell asleep on his settee. With all that had been going on I had forgotten about my tummy and paws. Now as I lay there I remembered all about it. I tried to bite at the now not so white stuff. I had been biting for some time when Mum saw me and told me to stop so I didn't manage to bite much of it off. To make sure I didn't bite at it any more Mum called me to lie at the side of her for a cuddle. I got myself comfortable. Mum kept stroking my ears, which was very nice. I lie back and fell fast asleep.

Mum had to put new white things on my paws because I nearly got them off a couple of times. When I saw under the white stuff, my claw was gone and in their place were things Mum called stitches. I tried to bite at them, but Mum gently tapped me on my nose and said, "No, Jenny, you mustn't touch, but you can have a look." Then she covered them back up again.

Some days later Mum and Dad took me back to the vet man to have my stitches out. I think that meant I wouldn't have them any more. Mum held me while the vet took the white stuff off. Then I felt some pulling on my paws and it hurt, so I cried out. Mum kept stroking my head and talking to me. "There, there, Jenny, be a good girl. It will all be done soon." Well, soon wasn't quick enough for me, so I *snapped* at the vet man. Well, he hurt me; wouldn't you have snapped? I didn't get near enough to touch him, though.

Mum said, "Jenny, really, don't you do that again." Then she tapped me on my nose to show me she wasn't having that. The vet man wrapped a thing around my snout! He wanted to show me he wasn't going to let me do it either. I felt silly with the thing around my snout, but I couldn't do anything about it now, could I? I just sat there in disgrace until it was all finished.

I was glad to get out of that place, but the whole thing was over now so things could get back to normal. Back at home Mum gave me some of my chocolate and a bit of a fuss, and I thought she was cross with me! "You were a good girl really, I don't blame you for snapping – it must have hurt a lot – I think I would have snapped too!" It was good to get rid of the white stuff and after a short while I forgot all about my tummy and paws and just got on with everyday life.

A few weeks later Mum told Dad it would be my first birthday at the end of the week. I didn't understand much about it, but I did get a special dinner and some chocolate. Mum also made a thing called a birthday cake, and I was allowed to have some of it – well, it was *my* birthday! Mum said she couldn't believe I was a year old and was now a big girl, so I must do more of that training I did before. Mum also said she couldn't imagine life without me now – that's nice. I couldn't imagine being without Mum and Dad, and our nice new home too. I had got through yet another obstacle in my life, that of going and staying with the vet man without Mum or Dad. To be quite honest, I wouldn't want to do it again, either...

CHAPTER EIGHT

THE WEATHER WAS STARTING TO GET WARMER and I spent a lot of time in the garden when it was warm enough for Mum to leave the door open for a while. Mum wasn't too well at times; she was having a lot more of that pain in her back. I think this pain hurt her leg too because she limped a lot of the time. I did all I could to help her. When she lay on the settee I would push myself as far under her legs as I could. By doing that Mum said it took the weight off her back and she said my warm body was very soothing, whatever that may be! Mum tried to keep smiling, but by the end of the day, after she had been to work and done the dinner for herself, Dad and me, the pain would be very bad and she became quieter in the evenings before bedtime. I think she was glad really when we went to bed.

When in bed, Mum would lie on her side and I would lie in her back with my tummy against her. This would give her some support and comfort her, so she told me. Mum would say, "Oh Jenny, that's wonderful. You are a good girl helping Mummy." Sometimes I would hear her crying in bed. That upset me so I would push myself even tighter into Mum's back and as I lay with my head on Mum's pillow, I would lift my head and kiss her ear just to show her how much I loved her. Mum liked that a lot; she would say, "Jenny, what would I do without you?

You make me feel so much better," while she stroked my back paw which lay by the top of her leg. I tried to help Mum as much as I could. I would have done anything to make Mum's pain go away. Dad loved her too, but he was too big to lie under Mum's legs and support her back in bed. I am sure he would have done, though, if he could.

One bright sunny morning I had been in and out of the garden enjoying the fresh air when I noticed the gate was slightly open. Dad had gone off to a place called church; Mum didn't go with him anymore because it hurt her sitting all that time. I should have told Mum that Dad hadn't shut the gate properly, but instead, I put my paw around the open bit and pulled it open enough to get through.

What an adventure I was going to have, I thought as I trotted along the path and grass. I didn't know many of the places around where we lived because we hadn't lived there long, as you know. Now I would have a good look around and see lots of new things. I felt quite excited as I saw new places and sniffed at new things along the way.

I had been going for some time when I looked up and suddenly realised I didn't know where I was. I began to get worried. I paced up and down a path but I didn't recognise anywhere at all. In my panic I now ran across a very wide road. I know I shouldn't do that because Mum taught me to sit at the road until she told me to cross over, but I was so frightened! I was now in a big park-like place, but this park had some white, woolly type of animals in it that Mum had showed me once before. By now I was very frightened. I wanted my mum. Mum, would I ever see you again? Was Mum wondering where I was, was she looking for me? She couldn't walk very far, so she wouldn't come all this way! Mum, *Mum!* I called out. I was now crying; I wanted to go home, but which way should I go?

After a while I heard my name being called. It was my dad calling me from across the big wide road. I was so pleased to see him I ran all the way to meet up with him on my side of the big road. As I got within a few feet of him I realised that he might be cross with me, so I slowed down to a crawl and eventually, crouching, came to a stop with my tummy nearly touching the floor. To help my case even more, at Dad's feet I rolled over onto my back and put my paws into the air – total submission!

Dad said, "Well, Jenny, you have been very naughty. I've been looking for you for ages. Mum wouldn't let me have my dinner until I went back with you. You're all muddy too. I don't know what your Mum's going to say when she sees you." Oh dear, Mum's not given Dad his dinner; he must be very cross with me. It's a good job I crawled on my tummy to him.

I trotted at Dad's side, now with my lead on. I hadn't realised how far I had gone until Dad took me back home. We reached the back gate. I was so pleased to be home again and be with Mum. Dad opened the back door and there stood Mum! "Jenny, where on earth have you been? I've been worried sick about you." I was sorry I had made Mum sick; it's not nice being sick, is it? I crawled up to Mum as I had done with Dad. I did want to jump all over her and smother her with kisses because I was so pleased to see her, but I thought the crawl approach would be a better idea. Mum's voice changed from shouting at me (I think she shouted because she was worried) to a soft, gentle voice. Mum dropped to the floor on her knees and she started to cry. "Jenny, I was so worried. I thought I would never see you again. I was at my wits' end."

I didn't know where "wits' end" was, but judging how worried Mum was, it must have been a long way. I wasn't there anyway, so there was no point in her looking there for me. By now Mum had her arms all around me and I was jumping up and down. Then all of a sudden Mum stopped and said, "Jenny, you are wet." Then she looked at me. "You're all muddy too. Well, it's too late now. You are going to need a bath, and so am I." Mum put her arms around me again and kissed me saying, "Don't you ever do that to me again. I thought I had lost you for ever." Then Mum started to cry again. We were on the floor cuddled up together for what seemed ages. Dad broke us up by saying, "Well, can I have my dinner now? I'm starving! It will soon be time for tea." I felt hungry too. After all, I had been on a very long walk and worked up a very hungry tummy.

The twist of this story is the fact that me and Mum were so dirty we needed a bath. The thing is, Mum liked having a bath, whereas I didn't. As far as I was concerned, water was only meant for drinking! I got my punishment – it was having that bath. I wouldn't be doing that again in a hurry.

A few weeks later it was very windy and the fence that goes around our garden fell down. Now, if I wanted to I could get out without using the gate. I went up to the edge of the gap and leaned out, but I didn't put my paw outside our garden at all. It would take, Mum said, a couple of weeks before the men could come and put up a new fence because the men were very busy. Mum told me that a lot of people had had a fence come down in the gales (that's what they call all of that wind), and even trees had come down. To be honest, although I enjoyed my adventure to begin with, I was very frightened when I was lost. I wouldn't want to do it again. In fact, I didn't like it at all with the gap in the fence, because although I could see out, people passing by could watch me when I needed to do my wee-wee. I didn't mind Mum seeing, but not other people! I was so pleased when the fence was all mended again. Although I never stepped outside, Mum would never let me stay out in the garden on my own, just in case I went out or children walked past and teased me. One thing that did change was the fact that whereas before I only wore my collar when I was taken out, I now had to wear it all the time because it had my name and address on it. As Mum said, you never know what might happen, do you...?

CHAPTER NINE

THE WEATHER BECAME A LOT WARMER AND I enjoyed going out for walks with Mum, although she didn't take me on long walks like she used to because of her leg. The back door was open from early morning until late afternoon. I could go in and out whenever I wanted to. I didn't stay out for too long at a time because it was cooler in the lounge room. When I did stay out longer I would pop in to see Mum, just to see if she was all right and to say hello, then go out again. Sometimes, in the afternoon, Mum would come outside with me and sit on the grass. I liked that; we would play ball together or just lie on a blanket and cuddle each other.

Mum and Dad started to talk about going on holiday to Wales and staying in someone else's flat. Mum said she would only go if I could go too, so they found a flat where dogs could go. I didn't understand why we would leave our house, to go and stay in someone else's house, just for one week, then go back home again. What was the point of it? But if Mum and Dad were going, I wasn't going to stay here on my own. I thought we would be going within the next few days the way Mum and Dad were talking. Mum then said, "Jenny, in a couple of months' time we will be at the seaside and you will love it."

I didn't know how long a couple of months were but I was now looking forward to this seaside thing!

Life carried on much as normal. Mum did all-day work again, so if she didn't have a day off I went to work with Dad. I liked it best when I could be at home with Mum. I could go in and out of the garden when I wanted to, and Mum would talk to me all the time. We would have a cup of tea and a biscuit together in the mornings and afternoons. In the afternoons too Mum would get on the floor with me and have a run-around playtime, which was good fun.

When I went to work with Dad I was left on my own a lot in Dad's room and I couldn't go outside until Dad took me. When it was lunchtime I went into the big room where the men went to eat their sandwiches; there were four to six of them at any one time. I had my dinner in Dad's room, but the men would always give me some bits out of their boxes, which was nice. I never asked for any bits because Mum would have been cross with me if I had done; the men would call me and give me titbits without me asking. Sometimes, if Dad wasn't too busy, he would take me from the porters' rooms to a place where old people sat making things. I liked to go there because I got a lot of fuss and met a lot of new people. I had the best of both worlds by staying with Mum and going to work with Dad too – can't be bad, can it?

One day Mum said she was going to do some packing and would I like to go upstairs and help her. The last time Mum did some packing we moved from the flat to our new house. I hoped we weren't moving again. I liked it where we lived now. I ran upstairs in front of Mum and jumped onto the bed. "We are going on holiday on Saturday so I must pack some things ready to take with us," Mum said.

Mum put some clothes for herself and Dad, towels and other things that she said we would need into our big bags. Mum didn't pack anything of mine though, because she said my things would have to go in bags at the last minute. When Mum had packed the bags I helped her to push them through to the box room so they wouldn't be in our way. Mum seemed pleased to be going to this seaside place. I wasn't too sure because she said there was a lot of water there called the sea! As you know, I don't like water.

Saturday arrived and Dad put all our bags into the car while Mum packed the last bits and pieces, including my bowl, towel and brush. Mum said I would need my brush to get the sand out off my coat. Why this sand stuff would get into my coat is a mystery to me, but there you are. I didn't ask. I was very excited now; I would just wait and see.

Everything was now in the car. Mum and me got ourselves into the car while Dad locked the front door, and then we were off and on the road to Wales.

We were in the car for some time when Mum said we would stop at the nearest place and have a cup of tea and I would be able to do a wee-wee. While Dad took me for a wee-wee Mum got out a little cooker thing and made the cup of tea. By this time we needed a break, but there wasn't anywhere for Mum to do a wee-wee. After all, she couldn't do it on the grass like me and Dad (he went behind a bush). Dad said he would stop at the next service station where he would get some petrol – that's food for the car – and Mum could do her wee-wee there. If we don't put the petrol stuff in the car it won't work apparently.

After our little break we all got back into the car

and carried on until we found a service station. I wasn't allowed to get out of the car because it wasn't safe. The next time we stopped Mum and Dad went to a place to have lunch. I had to stay in the car again because I'm not allowed in the food places. Before Mum left me she put my dinner and drink in my dishes at the back of the car on a towel so I could have my dinner while they were having theirs. When they came back they said it wouldn't be too long before we got to the seaside.

We eventually arrived at the place where we were going to stay. A lady came out and gave us a key so we could get into the flat. I was very excited now, but I couldn't see any of the water and sand stuff Mum had talked about. Well, I didn't think I could anyway, but I didn't really know because I didn't know what I was supposed to be looking for, or even how big it was. I think Mum would have told me if we had seen it though, because she always shows me things and tells me what they are. Mum and Dad took all the bags from the car and put them into the flat. The flat had a kitchen, one bedroom and a big lounge room that also had a bed in it. There wasn't much furniture stuff like at home, but there was a TV talking box. When everything was sorted out Mum made us a drink and said we would go out for a walk afterwards.

Off we went. We were told the way to get to the beach, (that's where the sand and water are). I was excited and I eagerly pulled on my lead. Mum said if I wasn't careful I would pull her over. We were only walking for a short while when Mum said, "There you are, Jenny, there's the beach." As she said it she picked me up so I could see over a wall that was twice my height. I couldn't believe what I saw. Next to the wall was the sand stuff Mum had told me about and beyond that was the water which Mum called the sea. This sea went as far away as I could see and it touched the sky. I looked both ways too, and I couldn't see the end of this thing called a beach. There were a lot of people on the sand and at the edge of the sea. They didn't go into the sea too far. Mum told me the sea got deeper as you went further out. I didn't know whether or not I wanted to go in the sea, but the sand looked nice.

We walked along by the wall, then went through a gap, down a slope and eventually we were walking on the sand. The sand was very soft and my paws went quite deep but it felt nice; it was warm too. Mum took her shoes off because she found it difficult to walk. This sand was light in colour and uneven where people had walked and children played. We started to get closer to the sea, and as we did the sand got darker and harder – in some places there were puddles!

Each time I came across one of these puddles I naturally walked around them – after all, I didn't want to get my paws wet, did I? Mum went through as many puddles as she could find and she tried to get me to do the same. She had no chance. Dad didn't go in puddles either. Well, he couldn't really, he still had his shoes on!

In the evening we went back to the flat. I was given my dinner and a drink; Mum and Dad had a meal they bought at a shop and took home to eat. It had been a long day. I was tired and fell asleep as soon as I got into bed, but I did need the sand taking off my legs and paws first.

The next day we were up early. I thought we would be going down to the beach but it was raining. Mum said we would go out in the car to see all the countryside instead and would stop somewhere for lunch. Mum took my two dishes, with some water and my lunch. I would stay in the car while they had their lunch. We drove around for ages. Mum kept pointing things out to me, so I didn't get bored. Eventually Dad drove up to a place where they would have lunch. Before Mum and Dad left for lunch Dad took me for a short walk so I could do a wee-wee while Mum sorted out my lunch and water, just like before. After a while they came back, but before we drove off we walked around what was called "the local beauty spot". It was very nice and it had stopped raining by then. We were back at the car after about an hour or so. Mum put me back into the car and then they left me while they went back to the place where they had had their lunch for a cup of tea before driving back to the flat. As Mum and Dad had a good lunch Mum did sandwiches for their meal. We stayed in the flat in the evening. It was tiring being in the car all day.

The next day was a sunny day but not too hot. Mum called it weather for walking out in. It was decided that today we would take a walk along the beach. The beach was very long and it would take all the morning to walk it. Mum made sandwiches and a flask of tea. I had my own meal and a bottle of water. My dishes and dinner were put in the bag with all the other bits and pieces Mum thought might be handy. We made our way down to the beach. There weren't many people about. Mum said it wasn't really warm enough for people to just sit about on the beach. As there weren't many people about Mum let me off the lead so I could run about and explore a little as long as I didn't go too far. To my surprise Mum got my ball out of her pocket and we played throw and fetch. Dad threw the ball sometimes too, but he threw it too far.

After what seemed ages we came to the end of the beach. We looked around for a nice spot to have our lunch. To be honest I was ready for a sit-down. I was very hungry and thirsty after all that walking, so were Mum and Dad I think. We stayed at this place for a while after lunch. Mum said I could run about without my lead as long as I stayed where she could see me. Believe me, I wasn't going to loose sight of Mum and Dad, because I didn't want to get lost, did I?

I only went a little way away, but it was nice to be free of the lead. All of a sudden I could smell something in the sand. I started to dig – it was good fun. I put the sand in a big pile behind me. The sand piled up so high I had to turn around and dig the other side. I could see something: it was white and long, like a stick but it didn't smell like a stick. I was now very excited. I dug harder. I had to find out what it was. I really enjoyed myself. The white stick thing was now within my reach. I pulled on it and all of a sudden it popped out! It was part of a bone! I got it in my mouth and ran back to Mum to show them. They laughed; they had been watching me all the time. I showed them my bone and I jumped around squeaking and barking with delight. I wagged my tail so much I thought it would drop off. "Look, Mum," I said, "don't you think I am clever? Look what I have found." Mum and Dad laughed. They seemed very proud of me, and why not – who wouldn't be? I carried my bone all the way back down the beach. People looked at my bone and smiled. I think they liked it too.

We got home and Mum and Dad had a cup of tea while I went to the garden to do my wee-wee and then I had a long drink too. I had my meal, then Mum had to give me a good brushing to get all the sand off my paws and coat. There was a lot of it on the floor when she had finished. Dad then got the car out and we all went to the place where they were going to have their meal. I would have to stay in the car, but I could see them through the window so I felt safe. Back at the flat we all went to bed early so we would be ready to go out again the following day. Believe me, we were all very tired. We had walked a very, very long way, and now I had a bone too.

For the rest of our holiday we had wet weather so we went "out and about" in the car seeing lots of new places and snatching little walks when the rain eased. We did manage one more trip to the beach but it wasn't very warm. As I went around the puddles I was suddenly surprised. Dad came up behind me, picked me up and ran over to the edge of the sea and put me down in it! It was so cold and I didn't like being wet so I ran back to Mum as fast as I could. I shook the water from my paws as I ran. Mum laughed and dried my paws with a paper thing she keeps in her pocket. Dad said he thought I would like it if only I would get the first dip over with. He was wrong. I didn't want the first dip – in fact, I didn't want to dip at all. I didn't like it and I never will. I will hate it even more now. After a while I forgave him, but I never let him come behind me while I was near the see ever again.

It was a good week. We had seen and done a lot of different things. Mum packed our bags again and we went back home. As we were getting nearer home I began to recognise where I was and got excited. Mum let me sit on her lap at the front of the car for the last part of our journey home. I ran from the car to the front door, wagging my tail and squeaking. I waited for Dad to unlock the door, then I rushed into the house. It was good to smell the familiar smells of our home. It was nice to go and see all those new places and do different things but it was good to be home again. Dad unlocked the back door and I ran around the garden, smelling everywhere. I had to make sure no one else had been in my garden while I was away. It was nice to do my wee-wee in private, in my own garden again. It was also a relief because I was getting desperate by now. Mum and Dad took the bags upstairs and then Mum made a drink while Dad put the car away.

It was early evening. Mum got something to eat for herself and Dad and put my food and drink down for me. We were all glad to go to bed. We had been in the car for a long time and were all very tired. You can't beat your own bed, can you? I snuggled up to Mum and soon fell fast asleep.

CHAPTER TEN

THE FOLLOWING YEAR AFTER HAPPY CHRISTMAS, Mum's back and leg gave her a lot of pain again. she put up with it for a long time. She would cry a lot in bed, so I would comfort her as best as I could. Even with me lying in her back it still hurt her a lot and she would cry. Eventually Mum went to see the people's vet man; he was called a doctor. When Mum and Dad got home Mum was upset and Dad started to bring our bed down to the lounge room. Mum cried, "I thought my days of bed rest were over. Now it's all starting again, when will it ever all end?" I comforted her as best I could, but I think she was tired and in a lot of pain.

Days were different now. Mum didn't go to work. She lay flat in bed most of the day and night. I stayed on the bed with her so she didn't get lonely. Mum did get out of bed to do her wee-wee and to let me out into the garden so I could do mine. She also fed me and gave me drinks. Sometimes Mum would get up and clean the floor and carpet, but she wasn't supposed to do that. After what seemed weeks Mum said she was going to a place she called a hospital that would take her pain away. The problem was, Mum would be away for some time, about two weeks, and I wouldn't be able to see her at all. I would miss her a lot, but if they were going to make Mum better I would cope. I would go to work with Dad every day so I wouldn't be alone.

Jenny, Her Own Story

The day came for Mum to go into the hospital. She should have gone in a thing called an ambulance but there wasn't one for Mum to use. Dad put Mum into the back of a friend's van on a thing called a stretcher which meant she could travel lying down. They borrowed the stretcher from the place where Dad worked. I was left on my own as Dad and the van with Mum in it drove off. I suddenly felt alone. I cried – I didn't want Mum to go away. Time would go slow for me until Mum would be home again, but I would be good, because Mum would be upset if I wasn't.

The days dragged while Mum was away. I didn't even feel like eating much. I was at work with Dad through the day. In the evening, before bedtime, Dad would go to see Mum so I was alone every evening until he returned. I wanted to go and see Mum too, but I wasn't allowed in that hospital place.

One day, about two weeks later, Dad got up earlier than usual and tidied up the house. We had our midday meal, then Dad went off in the car and I was left on my own again. After a while Dad came back but stopped the car at the front door instead of putting the car in the little car house. I couldn't see all of the car, but I think there was someone else sitting at the front. Dad came in on his own and did a strange thing. I jumped up to greet him but he went straight through to the kitchen and unlocked the back door. He called to me and made me go into the garden. Then he shut the back door and I couldn't get back in again.

After what seemed ages (I don't suppose it was really), Dad opened the back door and let me in again.

I knew something had happened, I could sense it. I felt excited but I didn't know why. I went into the lounge and guess what I saw? Mum was lying flat on the bed! Well, I went mad. I jumped onto the bed squeaking, and I kissed Mum all over her face. I was so pleased to see her. Perhaps you can understand how I felt. I thought my heart would burst with happiness because it was beating so fast. Mum hugged and kissed me saying, "Jenny, oh Jenny, I have missed you so much!" Mum started to cry. I started to cry and then Dad joined in too! There we were, all three of us, lying on the bed holding each other and crying. It was wonderful, as you can imagine. Dad then got up and made us all a cup of tea. He brought in a big bunch of flowers like Mum has in the garden. I never left Mum for the rest of the day apart from, that is, doing my wee-wee, and Mum had her arm around my all the time.

I had to be careful not to bounce on the bed because it seemed to hurt Mum. The next two weeks Dad stayed at home because Mum had to be careful and rest throughout the day. I didn't leave Mum's side for any longer than necessary. I suppose I was worried in case she went away again; anyway, I had to make up for lost time. Dad went back to work and life started to get back to normal.

After Mum had been back to see the doctor man she asked Dad to take the bed back upstairs again. Mum didn't go back to work again; she stayed at home all the time. I think she wanted to go but she wasn't allowed to. I liked her to stay at home with me, but that's not fair on Mum is it! Mum liked to look after people. She liked looking after me and Dad but it wasn't enough. She wanted to look after those old people like Granny and Grandpa. After a lot of weeks Mum's back was a lot better and it only hurt when she shouted out. Mum told Dad that a bit of her "scar" was tender and sometimes she had a sharp pain. I think the scar must be like the thing I have on my tummy. I couldn't understand it because my scar didn't hurt at all, so why did Mum's?

Mum went to some shops and came back with something called wallpaper. I didn't really understand because walls are not made of paper and anyway, why would Mum and Dad want paper walls? A few days later Mum and Dad moved some of the furniture into the middle of the room, and I wondered what was going to happen next! Dad went off to work and Mum started to put some thick, clear liquid onto the walls with a big flat brush. Mum said, "Well, Jenny, at least I haven't got old wallpaper to get off before putting up the new paper."

I couldn't see the point of putting that clear jelly stuff on the walls because when it was dry the walls didn't look any different to me. Mum must know what she is doing though. When Mum had finished putting that stuff on all the walls, she got a long, narrow table out. Then she got some very big scissors that she uses when she cuts out stuff on the floor, called material that she makes things like clothes with. There was a big bag that had rolls and rolls of that wallpaper stuff in it. Mum measured the wall and got a long, thin piece of wood which she then used to measure how much of the wallpaper she needed at a time. I thought that whatever Mum was going to do was very complicated and I couldn't understand the point of it all really.

I got a bit fed up with all this. Anyway, I didn't like things to be different. I went into the garden for a long time and left Mum to it. When I went back in to see what Mum was doing I had a big shock. Half of one wall had flowers all over it. How did Mum put them there? Mum said, "What do you think, Jenny? Do you like the wallpaper? Don't you think it makes the room look nice?"

So that's what wallpaper is – it's pretty flowers on a roll that makes the room look nice. It did look nice I must admit. I sniffed it but it didn't smell very nice – well, not like flowers, anyway. I wagged my tail and kissed Mum, then went back out into the garden.

Two days later Mum had put the wallpaper on all of the walls and put the furniture back in its proper place. The room looked clean and bright. It was much nicer than the plain not so white walls we had before. I was glad everything was back to normal again. I hoped this upsetting of our routine wasn't going to become a habit though.

A few weeks later Mum was getting fed up again, I could tell. Every so often she would get upset because she missed the old people, but I think it was more than that, though. Mum and Dad started to shout at each other sometimes. Mum was worried about something called money. She said that we would have to make a few cuts in the food bill. Mum said there would be no more expensive biscuits or cakes; she would make them all herself. Mum spent a lot of time in the kitchen making cakes, biscuits, meat and fruit pies and lots of other things. They were very nice. In fact Dad said they were better than bought ones, and I agreed with him. He said he didn't want Mum to go back to work again because he would miss all her cooking. I don't think Dad understood what work meant to Mum though. I did. She was happier when she had her work. I knew and understood when she was sad. Mum sometimes sat and talked to me about it and she would sigh and sometimes cry. I would just sit and listen and kiss her to make her feel better.

Although Mum was doing all this extra cooking, it wasn't enough for her to do because she liked to be very busy and be what she called "useful". One day Mum came home from shopping with more wallpaper stuff. "I'm going to decorate the kitchen next week, Jenny," Mum said. Oh no, not mess again, I thought, I hate mess and change. If it made Mum happy, though, I didn't really mind. The mess wasn't too bad really, and it looked nice when it was finished. I wondered which room would be next and what would Mum do when all the rooms were decorated. It was coming up to Happy Christmas again though, so that gave Mum lots of extra work to do. Maybe she would do more after Happy Christmas. I would just have to wait and see!

CHAPTER ELEVEN

ONE DAY NOT LONG AFTER Happy Christmas, Dad's auntie came to see us. I like Auntie Vi; she gives me fuss. I've been to her house where there are lots of fields like the one I was lost in. Mum made a cup of tea and then we all went into the lounge where Mum and Auntie Vi talked. After a while Mum screamed, jumped up and cuddled Auntie Vi. She screamed so loud it made me jump. I wondered what was wrong. I heard Auntie say, "It's only for three weeks but they might need holiday relief in the summer." I wondered what it was all about. It must have been good because Mum looked happier than I have seen her for some time.

"The main thing is," said Auntie, "there is no lifting so your back will be all right. Talk to Ian about it and then ring the home to let them know what you decide."

That gave me a clue – I think Mum's got a job again. I hope that doesn't mean I will be left on my own. Maybe I will go to work with Dad all the time from now on. If it makes Mum happy then it must be a good thing. Mum talked to Dad about it when he came home from work and he said if that's what Mum wanted he wouldn't stop her.

About a week later Mum and Dad went to see the home where the old people lived. When they came home Mum was so happy. "Jenny, next week I will start work at a home for old people. We will go at night and come home the next day. It's only for three weeks and then we will stay at home again so it's not going to be for long."

"We," Mum said, so does that mean I get to go with her?

When it was the Monday evening Mum packed a bag with some clothes for Dad and other bits and pieces that she thought she might need. Then to my surprise she packed my dish and blanket. I was going and so was Dad!

We arrived at a large house and when inside we were shown into a room that had two beds in it. I was left in the room while Mum and Dad went to meet the ladies. Apparently one of the ladies saw me when we first arrived. She told the other ladies and they all wanted to meet me. It was agreed that in the evenings I would go and see the ladies while Mum did some jobs, but stay in our room while the breakfast was being served.

The ladies liked it when I went up to them for a bit of fuss. I heard one lady say she had to give her dog to someone else to look after because she went to live in the home and she missed it a lot. The lady cried when she told us, saying that she had not even heard how her dog was getting on in his new home. That's terrible, don't you think?

The nicest thing about Mum's job was the walk home in the mornings, after she had finished all her jobs. Dad would take us in the car at night, but most mornings Dad had to leave early to go to work so Mum and me had to walk home. It was a long walk and a lot of it was through a very big park. It was the same park we walked through when we used to go and see how the house was getting on when it was being built. I was allowed to run around without my lead through the park.

When we got home Mum would do bits of cleaning and then we would have a cup of tea. After our drink we would go to bed for a few hours. It seemed funny going to bed after morning had started, but I was with Mum and that's all that mattered to me. On the days Dad didn't go to work we went home in the car, so I missed my long walk home with Mum.

At the end of the three weeks Mum was upset because she had enjoyed being, what Mum calls, "back in the swing of things again". That means she wanted to keep looking after the ladies. I think the ladies would miss Mum too, because on the last day they were very quiet while they were eating their breakfast. A funny thing happened while Mum was clearing up after breakfast. Several ladies came into our room, one after another. They told me to be quiet as they put something on Mum's bed. They gave me a bit of fuss, then left. They seemed upset too. Mum came in after a while; I think she was crying. I ran to her and gave her a kiss.

When Mum saw all the things that had been put on her bed she did cry. "Oh Jenny, I don't want to leave, I am going to miss coming here and seeing all the ladies." She kissed me and held me tight. Her face was against my head; my head was damp with her tears. I didn't know what to do so I stayed there, still. I occasionally gave her a kiss to tell her I understood, and believe me, I really *did* understand as I would miss it all too. Mum wiped her eyes and put all the little presents into her bag and we left the room for the last time. The ladies said goodbye as we walked to the front door. Mum smiled and said, "Don't worry, I'll be back to see you all soon. You can't get rid of me that easy." With that we left and Mum didn't even turn around and wave like she normally did. She was now crying a lot.

We crossed the big road and got to the park. By now Mum was sobbing. She took me off the lead but I didn't feel like running around so I walked at her side. I would miss my walk home, especially the run in the park.

Mum made a cup of tea when we got home. I sat on the settee beside her as she opened all the little presents and cards (I didn't think it was Mum's birthday, or I would have got her something. Well, it's too late now). As Mum opened each card she cried more and more. "It's a good thing I didn't open all these things at the home, Jenny," Mum said. Mum phoned Dad and told him what the ladies had given her. Mum said maybe they would ask her back if they were short-staffed. After our cup of tea we went to bed and both fell fast asleep. We were both very tired.

Mum tried to get used to being at home again, but she found it difficult. Then one day the phone rang. It was the home. They were talking about being short of people to look after the ladies, I think. When Mum put the phone down she had a big smile on her face. "Jenny, I'm going to work at the home again," She said. I was pleased for Mum. I was also pleased for myself too, because it meant I would get some fuss from all those ladies and have my long walks home

Jenny, Her Own Story

through the park again. Dad was pleased when Mum told him. I think he knew that is what Mum really wanted.

A couple of days before Mum went to a thing called an interview, she was doing some washing up when she sneezed. As she sneezed she screamed out, "No!" Dad went running into the kitchen and saw Mum laying on the floor. I was very worried when I saw Mum. She didn't look very well at all. Dad went to help Mum stand up, but she screamed again so it must have hurt her somewhere. Eventually Dad carefully picked Mum up and carried her to the settee and put a pillow under her legs. Apparently Mum's back was bad again. Mum was crying. I tried to help her by lying under her legs, but the pillow was in the way. After a while Mum asked Dad to move the pillow so I could get up and help her. I helped more than the pillow because I knew what to do, the pillow didn't. I also kept kissing Mum's hand, and the pillow couldn't do that! That helped Mum more, I think, than the support of a pillow. Mum rested all day and struggled to get into bed at night. I helped by lying as tight into Mum's back as I could, but she still cried on and off all night.

The day came for Mum's interview and she could hardly move. Dad said she should phone the home and explain what had happened, but Mum wanted to work there so much she was determined (that's the word she used) to get there. Dad took her to the home and I couldn't go, but Mum said they wouldn't be long. I was very worried when they left; I paced up and down and kept looking out of the window. Dad had to go to work after dropping Mum off so Mum had to get another car to bring her home called a taxi.

After what seemed ages a car stopped outside. A lady who worked at the home helped Mum out of the car. Once inside the house the lady helped Mum to lie down. Mum was crying. As soon as Mum lay down I jumped onto the settee and lay under her legs to help her. The lady left and Mum sobbed a lot. I didn't know what to do. I just kissed her hand and stayed as still as I could. Dad eventually came home from work. As soon as Mum saw Dad she burst into tears again. Mum said, "It's not fair, I've lost the chance to be assistant matron now and it's all because of my stupid back." Although Mum was in a lot of pain I think she was crying so much because she really wanted that job.

The next day the doctor man came. Our bed was brought downstairs again and Mum had to lie flat all the time, just like before. After several weeks Mum went to see another man at the hospital place she went to before. I had to stay at home. After what seemed ages Dad came home but to my horror Mum didn't; Dad was on his own. I frantically ran from the back door to the front door, hoping Mum would come in one way or the other. Dad stopped me. "Jenny, Mum's not coming home. She has to stay at the hospital, she will be away for a few weeks." Dad started to cry. I was so upset I cried too. I wanted my mum. I could look after her better than anyone else because I knew what to do and they didn't. Dad cuddled me and I kissed him. Dad would be able to see Mum as much as he liked because he worked at that hospital now, whereas I couldn't see her at all. I went to work with Dad every day so I was in the grounds of the hospital, but not allowed onto what was called the "ward" (that was where all the beds were). I missed Mum so much I couldn't eat my dinner and I didn't want to go for a walk either. I just wanted my mum.

Mum had been in the hospital for a long time when one day I had a surprise. Dad took me from his office room for a walk around the grounds. The ward places were dotted around the grounds and windows and doors opened out onto the grass and the flower things. It was nice, but I wasn't really interested. Dad stopped outside one ward and called to a lady. The lady came and said hello to me then went away. All of a sudden she shouted, "*Now!*" Dad picked me up, ran across a corridor and took me into a room. Someone shouted my name – I knew that voice, *Mum!* It was Mum! I jumped out of Dad's arms onto a bed where Mum was shouting, "Jenny, Jenny, Jenny! Oh, my baby!" I went around and around in circles, squeaking and kissing every inch of Mum I could see. Mum eventually stopped me and she held me tight. "Oh, my baby, I've missed you so much," she said as she kissed me. It only lasted for a few minutes then I was taken away again. I struggled to get out of Dad's arms to get back to Mum, but I wasn't strong enough. I couldn't do it. I was taken away.

It was nice to see Mum, but I wanted to stay with her longer – well, I didn't want to leave at all really. I don't think I was allowed to go into that place though really, so I shouldn't complain. I saw Mum two more times before she came home. Mum was away in that place for what Dad called three months; believe me, that's a long time...

The day Mum came home I knew she was coming

because Dad made the house tidy and bought the biggest bunch of those flower things I had ever seen. Dad went off in the car to get Mum and I stayed at home. The car arrived back home after what seemed ages. I saw Mum sitting in the front seat. I tried to get to Mum by scratching at the front door (I am not supposed to do that, but I was excited), but I couldn't get out of the front door. Dad came to the front door, opened it and I tried to get out but he grabbed me before I could do it. I thought I would get to Mum now, but instead I was put in the back garden. After a few minutes Dad let me in and I ran to see Mum as fast as my legs would carry me. I jumped on the bed squeaking with delight. Mum, Dad and me all lay on the bed together for a while, just, well, being together...

CHAPTER TWELVE

THINGS WERE DIFFERENT WITH MUM NOW. BEFORE she could walk she had to pick up two stick-like things that clipped onto her arms. Her leg was bent and twisted and she also had a metal thing on it. I don't know why she had these things. She didn't walk very well at all, and it was slow. Maybe if she took those things off she would stand and walk better. After all, my paws hurt until the white stuff was taken off, didn't they? It makes sense to me.

When Mum got her clothes off at bedtime she had a big white thing around her that went from under her arms down to where her legs started. It wasn't made from the same stuff as mine because Mum's stuff was very hard; Mum couldn't bend at all. It must have been very uncomfortable for Mum and she didn't even take it off before she got into bed either.

After a few weeks the white thing had gone but Mum had to keep the other things all the time. She couldn't even get into the garden very easily any more because of the big step. Life would be very different for all of us now. Whatever happens I will always be there to help Mum. I hope, though, that she doesn't have to go away ever again.

A big difference was Mum didn't take me for walks anymore. I missed our walks through the park and my run-around without my lead on. Mum was upset too because she couldn't take me anymore; she loved our walks together. Dad didn't take me for many walks and when he did, it was always a very short one. Sometimes Mum would ask Dad to take me. She would say things like, "If you take Jenny for a walk, I will do the washing up." Most times that worked but other times I would jump up and down squeaking and running to and from the back door. At first that worked but as time went on Dad would just say, "No, Jenny, go and see your Mum," so I gave up after a while.

In the warmer weather Mum would leave the back door open so I could go into the garden whenever I wanted to. Sometimes Mum would sit in the doorway and throw the ball for me. We both enjoyed that and Mum said it was a good way to give me something called "exercise" to keep me fit. I don't know how Mum or Dad kept themselves fit. They never ran up and down the garden after a ball!

I felt sorry that Mum couldn't come and play in the garden with me because she loved being outside. We would play with the ball or I would play chase. Mum would try to catch me but as she got closer and closer I would jump out of the way and go in the opposite direction. We would play like this for some time. Mum said it was good to get our heartbeats racing for a while. I didn't understand about that, all I knew about it was that it was good fun.

Life carried on much the same. We got used to Mum walking with the stick-things. Sometimes at bedtime Mum would cry, I think she was sad that she couldn't do all the things she used to do. She also had a lot of pain still. I don't think Dad knew that Mum cried because she only did it when Dad was asleep. At times, when Mum couldn't sleep, she would get out of bed and crawl downstairs. She would sit on the floor in the kitchen and watch the busy road. I know this because if I thought she had been gone for too long I would go downstairs to see if she was all right. Mum would talk to me and tell me how she felt. I was a good listener. She would stroke me all the while she talked. I liked it and I think it felt good for Mum too, as she seemed to sleep when she got back to bed.

In the summer I couldn't lie in Mum's back for too long because it made us both too hot. I would lie on top of the sheet at the bottom of the bed, where Mum's feet didn't reach. If Mum heard me panting to cool myself down she would crawl to the bathroom and fill a beaker with water. Slowly and gently she would bring it to me by putting it on the floor and crawling up to it. She would hold the beaker steady on the bed so I could drink from it without it falling over. When I had finished drinking Mum would put some water on her hand and wipe it all over my head and face. It felt wonderful and it cooled me down so I could then go to sleep. This is the way me and Mum looked after each other. We didn't have to ask each other what we needed; we just knew.

Mum made up for the things she couldn't do in the usual way by changing the way she did them. That meant I didn't miss out on anything at all. In fact, I was with my mum more because she didn't go to the home anymore, she just looked after me and Dad now. We spent nearly an hour of every day together just talking and listening to each other. I think I knew Mum better than Dad did, but I don't think Dad knew that. Mum always seemed to work out any problems and carry on as usual. If she got stuck she would talk it through with me. Although we couldn't go for our walks anymore I think we both enjoyed our chasing at playtimes. I also loved the way Mum would talk to me and tell me any news or tell me things she was going to do. I know Mum missed going to work but she was always busy, so I don't know how she found time to work in the first place. As for me, I liked it better with Mum at home. It didn't matter to me that she couldn't walk properly anymore. She was still my mum and I loved her very much.

CHAPTER THIRTEEN

LIFE SETTLED DOWN INTO A NICE ROUTINE. I WAS enjoying being with Mum all the time, sharing our playtimes and our quiet times. I particular enjoyed our tea breaks. If I was playing in the garden Mum would call me and when I looked up she would lift her cup and point to it. I would then go running into the house to have my cup of tea. After my tea I would join Mum on the settee to have my biscuit. Mum would sit at the side of me, break the biscuit and dip it into her tea. It was very nice. I wouldn't eat it if it wasn't dipped in Mum's tea, because it just somehow didn't taste the same. This, in a way, made our tea breaks into a special shared moment. We both enjoyed this time together. After we had finished our tea and biscuits Mum would kiss me on the nose and say, "Back to work". I would kiss her in return and then we would go back to what we were doing before our tea. It's moments like this that made me and Mum very close.

I can remember one time a friend of Mum's came to see us. I greeted her in the usual way and then carried on with what I was doing. After a while Mum called me and showed me her cup. I went running in to have my cup of tea, then on to join Mum on the settee for my biscuit. To my surprise Mum's friend had brought herself and Mum a special thing they called a "cream cake". I knew what that was because I have had some before, and I liked it very much; even more than my biscuit, and I liked that a lot. Mum gave me a piece of her cake with some of the white stuff called cream. I gobbled it up so quickly Mum's friend laughed. "She's certainly enjoyed that cake," she said.

I was looking at Mum for my next piece when Mum's friend leaned over and gave me a piece of hers. I went to eat it but when I looked at it there wasn't a blob of cream on it. I sniffed at it, then looked up at Mum's friend as if to say, "Where's the cream?" Mum burst out laughing.

Mum's friend said, "What's the matter, why isn't she eating it?"

Mum said, "She's waiting for the bit of cream!"

Mum's friend started to laugh and I was given my bit of cream. Well, would you eat a cream cake without any cream? I enjoyed my tea break that day. Mum and her friend did too, I think!

As time went on Mum had more and more of that pain again. I did all I could to help her but sometimes even I couldn't help much. Mind you, Mum said just me being there was a big help to her. Mum had to go and see the big doctor men at the hospital place several times. I don't think they helped her because she cried sometimes when she got home. Mum's neck became bad, so one day she started wearing a white thing around it. This meant she couldn't put her head down so she couldn't see me if I stood too close to her. After a while we got used to it and more or less carried on as we had been.

One time Mum came home from the hospital place crying. She lay down on the settee and called to me. I jumped on the settee and pushed myself under her legs. Mum was still crying and I didn't know what to do to help her. Mum called to me while tapping her tummy. That meant I should slowly and carefully crawl onto her tummy until my face was next to Mums so I could kiss her and she could fuss me. While we fussed each other Mum would talk to me and tell me her worries. On this occasion Mum said she had to go into hospital and stay for a few weeks. The hospital was a long way from home and she would not be able to see me or even Dad very often. Mum didn't want to go and leave me. She said she had had enough of those places.

The day came for Mum to go into hospital. Dad put Mum's things in the car while Mum said goodbye to me. I wanted to go with them but Mum said I would be better off at home. I cried as they drove away. I didn't want Mum to go away again. I liked her being at home with me. Time dragged. I didn't even know what to do with myself.

Eventually Dad came back. I ran up to him; I was glad to see him but he looked tired and upset. Bedtime came. I was let out for my wee-wee. I got upstairs and got on the bed as usual but it wasn't the same with Mum not being there. I didn't sleep very well – all my thoughts were with Mum. I wondered if she would sleep well or would she have a bad night like I was having, especially as she didn't have me to lie in her back for her. What were those doctor people going to do to her now? I wished they would leave her alone so she could be back with me, at home where she belonged.

I went to work with Dad again but I felt sad. There

were no cup of tea times or play and chase games, but most of all, I missed Mum! Bedtimes were lonely. Dad did his best. He would help me onto the bed and kiss me goodnight, but that was that till morning. Mum always kissed me and stroked my head while she talked to me. Sometimes Mum would even quietly sing me *our* special song. I don't think Dad even knew we had a special song. There was no getting up and going downstairs either, because Mum wasn't down there sitting in the kitchen looking out at the busy road. Once or twice, when I had slept for a while, I would wonder where Mum was and, thinking she must be downstairs, go to be with her. It would only be when I got there that I would remember Mum wasn't at home. I think Dad missed Mum as well. We didn't even have our evening meal like we did when Mum was there.

Dad did go and see Mum one evening through the week, but I wasn't allowed to go. I waited for Dad to come home. Home felt empty and quiet while he was away. When he came back he had a smile on his face. "Jenny," he called as he came in the back door. I went running to meet him. "Guess what, Mum can come home for the weekend! I will fetch her Friday and take her back on Sunday," he was still smiling. "That's good, don't you think?" he said, as he patted me. I didn't understand about days, but I did understand the words "Mum" and "home". I was so happy I ran around in circles. I ate all my dinner for the first time since Mum went away.

The days passed slowly until one day Dad came home from work and said he was going to the hospital to get Mum. I had to stay at home again, but this time

I didn't mind because Mum would be coming back with Dad.

I waited for what seemed ages, then finally the car arrived at the front door. I looked out of the window and saw Mum sitting in the front seat. I ran to the front door squeaking. Dad came to the door and as he opened it he grabbed me before I could get near the car. I was put, as usual, in the garden until Mum was inside.

As I waited I wondered if she was as excited to see me as I was to see her. I was sure she would be though. Dad opened the back door and I rushed into the lounge. Mum was still sitting in the chair with wheels which she used for going out. Perhaps she couldn't wait to get onto the settee before I came in; that must be it. She doesn't normally stay in that chair any longer than she has too. I made all my usual noises as I ran up to Mum. Mum screamed, "Oh Jenny, I have missed you so much," as she held me tight. She held me so tight I could hardly breath. I kissed Mum's face until it was so wet it shone when the light was on it. Mum cried. She just kept saying, "Oh Jenny, Jenny, Jenny." My fur was wet with her tears, but they were happy tears so I didn't mind at all.

After a while we had a cup of tea and a biscuit. I thought Mum would get out of her chair with the wheels and sit with me on the settee but she didn';. she stayed in that chair. I was given my biscuit dipped in Mum's tea. It tasted good, I had missed that while Mum had been away. After tea Mum got onto the settee and lay down. Her back hurt her, I could tell. As soon as Mum was lying down I jumped onto the settee and lay under her legs to help her. Mum called to me and tapped her tummy so I crawled onto her very slowly and carefully. "Jenny, I've got something to tell you," Mum said in a quiet voice. This was going to be a serious talk, not like the way Mum had talked when she first came home. When I had settled down after our exchange of a kiss, Mum talked to me while stroking my head. "Jenny," she said, "Mummy's going to have to use the wheelchair from now on, I'm not allowed to walk anymore." I didn't really understand everything she said, but I knew the words "walk" and "wheelchair".

While Mum was talking to me she had tears in her eyes and they were sad ones this time. "Tomorrow I will have to train you so you will be safe around the chair. I don't want to run over you, do I?" Mum smiled and kissed my nose so I kissed her. "Don't worry," she said, "everything will be all right."

I'm not sure who she was trying to convince, me or herself. I lay on top of Mum for a long time. I felt she needed me close to her face rather than under her legs this time to comfort her.

It was bedtime and after my wee-wee I went to go upstairs. Mum got herself to the stairs in her chair then used her stick things to get upstairs as usual. It was good to be in bed with Mum again. I had my fuss and kiss, then got myself tight against Mum's back as I knew this would help her. After a short while I heard Mum crying. I lifted my head and kissed her ear. Mum put her hand back and gently tapped me to say she liked it. After a while we both fell asleep.

It felt good waking up with Mum next to me. After breakfast Mum said we would start my new training; I hadn't done any of that since I was a puppy. I didn't know that there was any more training anyone could possibly do. On and off during the day Mum would call me but make me go to her on the right side of the chair every time. After doing it all day Mum said I should never go behind the wheelchair but always come in front. Mum said by doing that she would be able to see me and not run over me. It was a bit confusing to start with, but Mum was patient with me and I got the hang of it by the end of the second day. By the third day I was getting used to the idea of Mum being in the wheelchair all the time. Maybe that's what she was trying to tell me the other day. It didn't matter to me because Mum was still Mum, walking or sitting in a wheelchair. I think it mattered to Mum, but Mum being Mum would cope with it. After all, she has coped with all the other things, hasn't she?

In the late afternoon Mum started packing bits and pieces again. "I've got to go back to the hospital for another week," Mum said. "I shall be home again on Friday so be a good girl for me and look after your Dad." I didn't know Mum was going back again. I thought she was home for good. Me and Mum cried as she went off in the car. It would be a long week again for both of us. I didn't know Mum had to go back to that place. It would have spoilt the time we did have together had I known. It was strange going to bed that night without Mum to settle me and sing quietly to me.

The following day I went to work with my dad again. I didn't eat my dinner; I didn't feel hungry. Dad shouted at me because I didn't eat it, but I don't think he felt very well. In the afternoon the telephone-thing rang its bell in Dad's office. Dad picked it up and said hello. After a short while Dad put the handle down and called me. "Jenny, Mum's coming home today. They say I can go for her after work." Mum and home; that's two words I really understand and that was enough for me.

Dad left work early because he had a thing called a cold. He put me in the car and we drove off. After a while I realised we weren't going home. We must be going for Mum, I thought.

After a very long time in the car Dad stopped outside a place that looked similar to where Dad worked. He left me in the car and after a short while he came back with Mum. I was shaking with excitement. I jumped around the car so I could see her as she gradually got closer. I don't think Mum knew I was in the car, because when she saw me she screamed with delight. I am sure, if she could have done, Mum would have jumped out of her chair and got into the car all by herself. We went through our usual greeting – it felt so good. Mum said they let her go home because they couldn't help her any more, as she had done so well with the wheelchair on her own. I could help her and I would, so it's better she comes home to me really. The best part of it was, Mum didn't have to go away again. Once home this time she can stay home. All I can say is, let's go home and have a cup of tea and, of course, one of Mum's biscuits!

CHAPTER FOURTEEN

ME AND MUM GOT USED TO THE WHEELCHAIR. I did get the end of my tail run over a couple of times in the first few weeks, but it was my fault. I shouldn't have been behind Mum at the time. Sometimes, after a cuppa, if Mum got close enough to the settee I could walk onto her lap. One time I did this, Mum started to push the wheels and we moved. I wobbled a bit but Mum said I would be all right, so I didn't jump down. After a short while I moved my weight from one paw to another so I could balance like I do in the car. I enjoyed it very much. Mum wheeled us over to the window and we looked out together. It was a lot easier than looking out with my front paws on the ledge. I gave Mum a kiss to show her I liked it. It was also nice to be able to sit on Mum's lap again, too. After that first ride, I got the hang of it and would jump on to Mum's lap from the floor. This was another way me and Mum could be close. We often sat like that, talking together and looking out the back door at the busy road.

After a couple of weeks, Dad laughed at Mum when she bumped into the side of the door. Mum said if he could do any better he should try and do it. With that Mum got herself to the edge of the seat and dropped on to the floor. "There you are, get in the chair and push yourself from one room to the other!"

Dad said, "It's easy," and he sat in the chair. As he

moved off and tried to get from the lounge to the kitchen, he bumped into the stairs and the edge of the doorway. He also kept putting his foot down to get the chair straight again. That's cheating, I thought, Mum can't do that, can she? Dad got fed up with it so he pushed it back to Mum.

"Not so easy as it looks, is it?" Mum said with a smile. Dad just grunted and asked when it would be dinner time.

Things carried on, as they do. Then one day I had a bit of confusion. You know Mum taught me to go to the front of her chair so she could see me? Well, she said, "Let's go into the lounge," and she went backwards! This meant when I faced Mum she was going away from me instead of coming towards me. Confused? Well, so was I. Mum said her arms hurt so she had to use her foot to help the chair move. She said it took too much strength to pull forward so it was easier to go backwards. Mum said we would have to re-train. That means I have to forget what Mum said about the chair and learn something new.

One day a lady came to see Mum about her wheelchair. The lady said Mum should have a powered wheelchair so she doesn't have to push herself any more. The lady said she would arrange it all and Mum would get a letter to tell her where and when to go and see about it. I didn't really understand how Mum's chair was going to move if she didn't push the wheels, but Mum understood and that's all that mattered.

A few weeks later, the letter came. Mum was very excited about it really. Dad arranged to have that day off so he could take Mum because it was a long way away. Mum said I could go with them and we could have a picnic. I liked picnics; we have had a few when it's been warm enough. That's when we eat sitting on the blanket on the floor.

The day came for us to go. Mum finished doing the picnic by putting my dish in her bag. We were in the car for a very long time and it was hot. We eventually got to the right place and Dad put the car under a tree so I would be cooler. Mum told me to be a good girl and then they went to a building nearby. I could see Mum and Dad inside the building through the window, so I didn't cry. After a while they came back but Mum was still sitting in her normal chair. I didn't understand; I thought Mum was getting one she didn't have to wheel herself. I suppose they know what they are doing. Mum said, "Now that's over we can have our picnic." As they put the blanket on the floor, I thought, Good, about time, I'm starving.

It was a long way back home. Although Mum had laid down on the blanket for a short while, she was still in a lot of pain. When we got home, Dad put me into the back garden so I could do a wee-wee. He kept the back door open so I went straight back in after I had done it. Dad was carrying Mum in when I got into the lounge; she was in so much pain, he put her onto the settee. As soon as Mum had settled, I jumped up and tucked myself tightly under her legs to help her. She was crying, but she told me I was a good girl for helping her.

After a few days, Mum was back to her usual self again. Time passed, then one day Mum had a letter on the front door mat. Mum made our cup of tea and while we had a biscuit, she read her letter. Mum said,

"About time too, Jenny. Next week my powered chair is coming. It will make my life a lot easier, won't it?"

I didn't know really because I couldn't understand how a chair could move if no one pushed it.

The day came for Mum's chair to come. It was mid-afternoon, just after cup of tea, when the bell on the door rang. Mum was excited and I was too, but I was excited for Mum not for myself. The man pushed a chair, smaller than Mum's, into the kitchen. That's no good, I thought, Mum wants one she doesn't have to push. Anyway, the wheels were very small; Mum would never be able to reach them. After the man put the chair in the kitchen, he left. Mum had to get onto the floor and sort it all out. She was a bit upset because some of the pieces didn't fit because they were for the wrong side of the chair. After sorting it all out, Mum folded up her normal chair and sat in the new chair. I think she liked it but I still wondered how she was going to wheel it, especially with those small wheels.

Mum said, "Right, Jenny, move out of the way so I don't run over you." I moved aside and sat to watch what Mum was going to do. Mum pressed a button and a light came on. She pushed a little lever and the chair moved forward really fast. I don't think that either of us were ready for that. Mum went from room to room by just pushing the little lever. Every time Mum stopped, the chair would make a clicking noise. Mum said the clicking noise meant the brakes were going on. That's helpful; I will at least know when Mum is going to stop.

By the time Dad came home, Mum was going from room to room with no trouble. Of course as soon as

Dad saw the chair, he had to have a go. He started going through the doorway and bumped into it, then he turned quickly and nearly ran me over. I had to run away from him a couple of times. In the end I had to jump onto the settee. If I hadn't, he would have run me over!

After a few days, you would think Mum had been using it for a long time. It made my mum's life a lot easier, by making her less tired and also stopped some of her pain. There was just one thing: I had to re-train yet again because Mum came towards me when facing me like the first time she used the chair. It was easy for me this time because I had learned it that way in the first place. Do you remember how I learned to jump onto Mum's lap with the old chair? Well, I soon learned how to do it with the new chair too. It was good. We went faster and smoother in this one. I liked it and I didn't even get my tail run over by it. Mum gave her new chair a name – she called him Bertie.

Things went well until one day Mum noticed white patches on the new lounge carpet. This really worried Mum because she said it was a thing called acid which must have leaked out of Bertie and Mum said acid burns. Mum got on the settee and called me, "Jennie, come and sit with me. I want to look at your paws." With that Mum picked up each paw in turn and looked at my pads. I don't know what she was looking for, but she was worried. "That's fine," she said, "but I will have to check them every day from now on, until I get Bertie sorted out." Mum then did a funny thing; she put some milk in a dish and, using a cloth, she rubbed the milk onto the carpet! I followed

Mum from one spot to another and I couldn't see any difference to any of the spots.

A few weeks later, Bertie was all sorted out because a man came and mended it. I'm glad Mum has this new chair because anything that helps Mum can't be bad, can it?

CHAPTER FIFTEEN

THE DAYS STARTED TO GET COOLER SO MUM would shut the back door by late afternoon. It had been a nice summer going in and out of the garden and playing ball with Mum. She would sit in the doorway and throw my ball. I would run after it and take it back to her. Mum couldn't get into the garden, but we both liked playing ball.

Day by day as it got colder, Mum said it was too cold to play ball outside any more. Mum worked out a way so we could still play by getting a softer ball that wouldn't damage the furniture. In the middle of each afternoon Mum would get on to the floor and put Bertie out of the way in the corner. We would start off by playing ball; Mum said it was a warm up, whatever that was. After a while we would play chase. That's where I dodge about and Mum has to catch me. I usually win, but sometimes I let Mum win, because that's only fair. This game is to get (so Mum says) our heart rate going fast. I didn't really understand; I just thought it was fun. We would finish by Mum doing something called physio and me doing my best to copy her. It was hard work but fun. Mum said we must do it to keep us fit.

Once every two weeks, I would be called upstairs to the bathroom. Mum would be on her knees with a thing called scales in front of her. I was taught how to step on and off these scales-things. Mum would look down at something called a dial. If the dial was in the same place as the last time, Mum would tell me how good I was. I would look down at the dial too, but I didn't know what I was supposed to be looking for. If the dial moved around further than before, Mum would say, "Jenny, you have put on weight. You will have to eat smaller meals for a while." Cut down on my food? That's not fair, I shall be hungry. As long as Mum doesn't cut out my biscuit, I will manage, I hope. When I had put on weight before, Mum just gave me less in my dish. I didn't even know my meals were smaller. We also had longer playtimes, but I don't know if that was anything to do with me putting on weight. I arrived upstairs and jumped on the scales. I looked at the dial, then looked up at Mum. Mum looked at the dial too, "Well done, Jenny, you are a clever girl. You haven't put on weight this time." I was so pleased I went running and jumping around. I didn't think I was clever though – I just did what I normally do, but if Mum was pleased, so was I.

Most playtimes we would also play a game which meant I would jump from one settee to the other. This entailed me sitting on one settee while Mum crawled across to me on the floor. I would sit with my front paws stretched out in front of me, my bottom sticking up in the air and my ears would be pricked up. Mum would then crawl up to me, sometimes slowly, other times she would quickly pounce on me. Before Mum actually got to me I would dodge around and jump onto the floor, then onto the other settee. Sometimes I would jump from one settee to the other. We would do the whole thing over and over again. It was very tiring but good fun, especially when she shouted a funny word like "*Boo!*"

We never got fed up; we had so many games to play. Sometimes I would start a game and other times Mum would. Dad didn't play games with me very often. When he did, it involved usually Dad sitting in his chair and throwing my ball across the room, then I would run to get it and take it back to him again. We would only do it for a few times, then Dad would say, "Go to your Mum and play." I didn't mind because I liked playing with Mum the best.

Most days, after playtimes, Mum would get my brush and groom me. This, so Mum said, was to relax us after all that chasing. I would lay on the floor and Mum would brush one side of me starting at my head and going down my back to the tip of my tail. I would lay there with my eyes closed enjoying the attention. Side one completed, Mum would gently turn me over and do the same on the other side. When Mum stopped brushing, I would turn myself over again to try and keep her doing it for a bit longer. Mum would laugh and do it all again; it was perfect bliss. Sometimes, when Mum had completely finished, I would be so relaxed I would fall asleep until it was time for our meal. I can say we really enjoyed our playtimes, but I think that it was due to Mum shouting and making that giggle noise all of the time. We always ended with a big cuddle which seemed to say playtime had come to an end.

CHAPTER SIXTEEN

LIFE CARRIED ON MUCH THE SAME FOR ME. I WAS lucky, I was well loved, had a really good Mum and Dad and plenty to eat. I also had plenty of treats and rides out in the car thing when the weather was good. Things weren't so good for Mum, though. Trying to crawl up and down the stairs was becoming very difficult for her. Mum would send me up first and then I would sit at the top and wait for her. When she first started to crawl upstairs after being at that hospital and coming out in the chair, she crawled up quite quickly and all in one go. Now Mum had to keep stopping and only go up a few stairs at a time. It gave her a lot of pain and was also very tiring too. Well, you try it and see for yourself. I can do it easy but I do have four legs instead of two and my legs don't hurt like Mum's, do they?

One evening, Mum had to go up and down the stairs so many times to do her wee-wee it made her very tired. All of a sudden when she was on the stairs I heard her cry out "Oh, no!" I ran to the bottom of the stairs the same time as Dad to see what was wrong. Mum was now crying... Dad asked her what was wrong and she said she had wet herself because she couldn't get to the toilet (that's where people do their wee-wees) in time. Dad went and sat down; I went up to Mum to comfort her. Mum still had to crawl up the rest of the stairs and get to the bathroom, so she could get herself clean again. I felt so sorry for Mum. I remembered how I felt when I had an accident like that; it wasn't very nice at all. I stayed with Mum until she went back downstairs into the lounge.

The following day, at cup of tea time, Mum said she would have to have a serious talk with Dad when he got home from work. We all had our dinner when Dad was home, then Mum asked Dad if they could talk. I sat on the settee and kept quiet because I knew this was important to Mum. Mum and Dad talked for quite a while, then Mum made a cup of tea and came to lie on the settee with me. I wasn't told what they had been talking about.

As time went on, Mum still had to struggle to crawl up and down the stairs. I knew there was something going on, though, because from time to time, people would come to the house and look at our stairs. One time a lady and two men came all at the same time and all stood at the bottom of the stairs talking. Nothing ever changed after these people had been, so I don't understand why they kept coming. After all, one set of stairs is much the same as another, I thought. Surely these people know what they looked like by now?

One day, after a long time, the man who lives with Mum's friend came with big boxes that he called a tool kit. After bringing his tool kit in, he started to make a hole in the top of the room under the stairs. It made a lot of noise and all bits and pieces of that stuff fell onto a sheet (like we have in bed) that the man had put on the floor before he started.

I was glad when he had finished and my settee was

put back where it belonged under the stairs. Mind you, every time I looked up now, I saw the big hole and I didn't like it. I always got a bit worried when my usual days were changed in anyway, especially when the disturbance is noisy and causes a mess at the same time. I did wonder why we had to have this hole and how long it would be there for. I hoped it wouldn't be there all the time; it didn't look very nice. I couldn't understand why it had been done really. I suppose Mum will tell me when she feels I should know.

Some time passed, then one day Mum started to move some of the things that were under the stairs. Later in the day, a man, whom I hadn't seen before, came with another one of those toolbox things. It wasn't the same one that Mum's friend had used, because this one was bigger. Oh no, I thought, there's going to be more noise and mess. I'm not going to like this at all, but it's a nice day, so I can at least go out into the garden to get away from it all. I don't think Mum liked all this upset to her day any more than I did. This man didn't stay as long as Mum's friend, and it wasn't as messy, but Mum still had to tidy up after he left. I couldn't see anything different to how it was before; the hole was there just the same. Mum said the man had put the electrics in.

Nothing seemed to happen for a long time, until one day the lady and two men came back again. This time instead of looking at the stairs, they all stood and looked at the hole! The mind boggles. I don't understand you humans sometimes – why stand and talk about a hole?

After looking at the hole they went on to look at

the rails that Mum and Dad hold on to when they go up the stairs. What were they going to do with these rails? Does this mean there is going to be more noise and mess? I hope not.

Nothing happened for ages. Anyway, how is the hole under the stairs and all the talk of the rails going to help Mum get up and down the stairs? If the stairs were shorter, they wouldn't reach the toilet and they can't be taken away either, or you couldn't get upstairs at all! I don't understand it. It's all very confusing.

Mum's friend came back again with his toolbox and he had two large pieces of wood with him (well, that's what the man called it anyway). By the time he had finished, the pieces of wood were down the side of the rails to block the gap up between them. I didn't like the look of it at all, and the wood was very dark. I went up the stairs that night to go to bed; the stairs were darker than before. I also didn't realise till the following morning that I could no longer see between the rails. I had to peep between the top and second rail because they hadn't been filled in like the bottom ones. It was a bit of a stretch to do that too, but I liked to look because I could also see through the lounge window from the stairs.

A couple of days later, Dad coloured the wood white with something called paint. I know it was called that because when Dad wasn't looking, I went up to it to smell it. Dad shouted, "Jenny, that's paint and you've now got it on your nose!" As I moved away, my eyes were drawn to look at my nose because there was a big white blob on the end of it. Mum came in with a cloth to try and wipe the blob off. A little came off, but Mum said the rest of it would have to wear off. Every time I woke up after a nap, my eyes were immediately drawn to that blob on the end of my nose. It took several days before it finally wore off.

One day Mum said she had something to tell me. "Jenny," she said, "come and sit on my lap." She tapped her knees with her hand. I jumped up, kissed Mum's nose and settled myself. "Tomorrow, some men are coming to put a stairlift in for Mummy. This lift has a seat for me to sit on and when I press a lever, the seat will take me upstairs," she said as she stroked my head. "It will be a lot easier for me and when you get used to it being there, you can ride on it on my lap sometimes. You will like that, won't you?"

I gave her a kiss as an answer, but I didn't really understand how a seat could take anyone up a lot of stairs. If Mum was happy, and she seemed to be, then I was happy. Does all this mean we are going to have some more noise, mess and disturbance to our usual routine again?

We were up early the next day, and shortly after, the men came. I spent most of the day in the garden, popping in to see Mum from time to time. At lunchtime, Mum called me in to have my dinner. After I had finished eating, I went to see what the men were doing. There was a shining thing, which took up about half a tail's length in width going up the wall side of the stairs. By my settee sat a large seat which was much wider than Mum's chair. This chair only had one leg under the middle of the seat. I wondered how it was going to stand up on its own. The men started work again so I went back out into the garden to get away from all the noise. Mum called me in after a short while as the workmen had left.

I expected to see a mess in the lounge, but everywhere was tidy. Mum showed me the "stairlift" thing. I gave it a good investigation – after all, I had to be sure it was safe for Mum to use, didn't I? Mum made the chair come down the metal thing by pressing a lever. It was quite noisy really. She sat on the seat, pushed the lever up and the chair started to go up the stairs. It made me jump, so I barked and ran around in circles. When Mum came down again, she patted her lap and called me to sit with her on the chair. I wasn't too sure so I barked and backed away. Mum laughed and said, "It's all right, don't worry, it won't hurt you. Maybe you can have a ride another day when you get used to it." With that, Mum got off the lift and got back in her chair, then gave me some fuss and a playtime to take my mind off it.

Every time Mum used the lift thing to start with, it made me jump, although Mum always told me when she was going to use it. When Dad came home from work he, of course, had to investigate it all just as I had done. He also had to have a ride on it, but he didn't just do it one time like Mum did, he went up and down a few times before he would get off!

What I didn't see earlier – well, not until I lay on my settee with Mum – was that the hole had gone from under the stairs. Instead of the hole there was now a big box thing dangling from the top of the room. I couldn't understand how it stayed up there. I was a little worried it might fall down on top of me. Mum wouldn't let that happen to me though, would she?

After a while, Mum told me she was going to use the lift. "Do you know, Jenny," she said, "I think I will call the stairlift Stanley. It sounds much better than the stairlift, don't you think?" I didn't mind what it was called really, because I wasn't sure if I was going to like it anyway. Maybe Stanley sounds more friendly and less frightening though.

Mum got herself to the stairs and called, "Jenny, I am getting on Stanley now." I was ready for the noise now I thought, but I was in for a shock! There was such a loud noise, it made me jump off my settee with such speed, I wondered where I was going. The noise didn't come from the direction of Mum's chair, it came from the big box above my settee. I wasn't prepared for that and it didn't seem that loud when I sat by the seat. After Mum came back downstairs, she gave me some fuss to calm me down. Mum came up with a plan to help me not be so afraid. She asked Dad to go and use Stanley while she sat on the settee with me to show me there was nothing to be afraid of. After Dad had been up and down the stairs a few times, while Mum sat and comforted me, I felt a lot happier about it all.

After a few days, when we were going to bed, Mum asked Dad to pick me up and put me on her lap so I could ride up with her. I wasn't too happy, and I struggled to get away. Mum talked to me and calmed me down. I sat on Mum's lap a while before she made it move and that was all right. When we did move off, I felt a jolt (a bit like when the car starts), but after that we smoothly, but slowly, were taken up the stairs. To be honest, after a few seconds I lost my fear and quite enjoyed it really. From sitting on Stanley too, I could also see clearly through the lounge window, which was very nice. We stopped with a slight jolt at the top of the stairs. I wasn't too sure as to what I had to do; I waited for Mum's instructions. Mum said, "Hold on, Jenny, I must turn the seat around first." With that the seat turned with me and Mum sitting on it. We were now facing the wall on the landing. Mum told me I could jump down, so I did, wagging my tail as I landed on the floor. I wasn't frightened of Stanley any more now. I didn't ride on him very often after that; instead I would go upstairs before Mum and sit at the top until she arrived. It made life a lot easier for Mum, and that helped her with her pain and what's good for Mum is also good for me.

CHAPTER SEVENTTEN

SEVERAL YEARS HAVE PASSED SINCE STANLEY arrived, but things have carried on much the same. I am with Mum every day and night. She hasn't been away to those hospital places either, which is good. We still have our play and cup of tea times. I just wish Mum could come and play outside in the garden with me, but she can't get down the step. Mum has more pain than she used to, so I help her more with that. Through the night, when Mum goes downstairs I sometimes go and sit with her, if she has been gone for a long time. I sit at her side and she strokes me as she talks. I listen to Mum telling me what she would like to do if only her body would let her. She tells me all the things she calls "secrets and longings". Mind you, I don't understand what "secrets and longings" are really. Whatever they are, Mum tells me not to tell Dad about them. We enjoy these special times together. I know and understand Mum's feelings and she knows mine; we are very close.

I am now, what I would be called in people years, getting on a bit. I am twelve, which is about eighty in your years. I am very well and fit for my age. That's due to my playtimes and also Mum keeps an eye on what she calls my weight, so I don't get fat. I do get little niggles with my joints and I do go off my food a bit when I just feel a little unwell. At these times, I get extra attention from Mum. She is so gentle and kind, it makes me feel better.

I remember one time when I felt unwell and a place near the top of my front leg, just down from the bottom of my neck, hurt. I had my playtime with Mum, but Mum realised I wasn't my usual self. "What's the matter, Jenny?" Mum said. "Come and let Mummy have a look at you."

I went up to Mum, my head down and my tail drooping with just a slight wag at the end of it. Mum said, "Oh, Jenny you feel hot. Let me have a feel over you so I can see if you have any pain."

With that Mum slowly and carefully started with my head, and feeling as she went, worked her way around my body. All of a sudden, I felt a lot of pain as Mum touched the spot that hurt. I whimpered to let Mum know that was the place that was causing me to feel poorly. "You stay there, Jenny. I'm just going to get your brush so I can move your fur away and see what's going on," Mum said as she went off. I did as I was told and waited for Mum to come back. Mum got herself out of her chair and back on to the floor beside me. Mum got me to lie on my side that didn't hurt, then she started to clear my fur from around the offending area. "Oh Jenny, you have a big lump. It looks like an abscess that's nearly ready to burst." I didn't know what an abscess was; I just knew it hurt and made me feel ill.

Mum said that she would have to try to burst it for me to get rid of some of the puss and then I would feel a lot better. I didn't understand what she was saying, but I knew Mum would do her best to make me feel better. "If it doesn't burst, we will have to take you to see the vet, so he can make it better," Mum said.

Vet! I don't want to go to the vet, Mum! I don't like him because he gives me those injection-things. I hope Mum can make me better.

Mum left me on the floor. "I won't be long," she said. After a while, Mum came back with a towel, some hot water in a dish (I know it was hot because steam stuff was coming from it), and something she called "cotton wool". As I lay there, Mum started to bathe my abscess" with the cotton wool dipped in the hot water. It was very painful. I cried. Mum kept talking to me and stroked my head with her other hand while she put another piece of hot cotton wool on the abscess. "I know, I know baby, Mummy will try and make it better. You are very brave." When Mum put the next piece of cotton wool on, all of a sudden the abscess burst! I gave out a big yelp – ooh, it was so painful! Mum called out "Oh my gosh, Jenny, that smells terrible! There's puss pouring out of it." I wasn't too worried abut the smell at first; I was just relieved that the bad pain had gone away. I now just felt a slight throbbing.

Mum started to clean up the sticky, smelly mess that had trickled all down my fur. As Mum cleaned me up, I lifted my head and kissed Mum's hand to say thank you. Mum leaned over and kissed my head. "You will start to feel better when all that poison is out of your system," she said, adding that I had been a very good girl.

Poison? What's poison? I thought it was puss that came out. No wonder I felt ill! When Mum had cleaned up some of the mess, she said, "I am sorry,

Jenny, but there's still a lot of puss in there. I will have to squeeze it to get more out and it will hurt, but I have to do it to make you better." Mum didn't like it any more than I did, but as Mum said, it had to be done! I did whimper each time Mum squeezed it, but I didn't move because I knew Mum had to do it. After a few goes, Mum said, "That will do for now. I think you have had enough for today. I will put a big pad of cotton wool on it and wrap a bandage around your body to keep it in place." I had to stand up so Mum could put the bandage on. It felt really funny, but I didn't mind because it was a lot more comfortable than it was before.

After all that, I was desperate for a wee-wee. I think Mum realised because she said, "I think you had better go and do a wee-wee, then when you come back we will have a cup of tea with a biscuit." Good idea, I thought, as I went out into the garden.

By the time I came in, Mum had cleared everything away and had made our tea. A while later, Dad came in and he said, "What on earth is that terrible smell?" Mum told Dad the whole story and he came up to me and gave me a bit of fuss. "Good thing it didn't burst in the middle of the night when we were in bed," Dad said. I was so glad it had burst too; it had been very painful.

For the next few days, in the afternoons, Mum took my bandage off and squeezed more puss out of the abscess. Then one day, no more puss came out, so Mum just put the bandage on without the cotton wool. Mum said she kept the bandage on so I couldn't scratch or nibble at it... Eventually, the bandage was taken off and all you could see of the whole affair was a little bald patch where Mum had cut my fur away. It was wonderful how Mum made me better and looked after me. I wouldn't want to go through all that pain and discomfort again, even if I did get more fuss! This shows how me and Mum looked after each other and how close we were through everything. Thank you, Mum!

CHAPTER EIGHTEEN

It has been a couple of years since my abscess and I have been quite well for my age. The only problem I have noticed is that lately I don't always hear when Mum calls me, especially when I am down at the bottom of the garden. When I am in the house, I don't always hear the front doorbell go or hear when people come in the back way.

I think Mum realised I had a bit of a hearing problem. When I was at the bottom of the garden, Mum would clap her hands together – that noise would make me look up towards the house. When Mum had my attention, she would either open her arms out wide, which meant she wanted me back at the house, or do what she called a roly-poly action with her arms, which meant come now and quickly. It only took a couple of these actions before I got the hang of it. Mum's clever to think of that, don't you think? And at least I can still come when she calls me. Mum also got her friends to call out when they come in, so at least I knew they were there. My deafness didn't seem too much of a problem because of the things Mum did to make life as normal as possible.

Mum helped me with another problem too. I went to work with Dad one day, because Mum had to stay in a place to have a rest for two weeks – she did that from time to time, but I didn't mind because I was allowed to go in and see her. I saw lots of other people who used wheelchairs like Mum and had a lot of fuss from them. I think they enjoyed my visits as much as I did.

On this particular day, I was having my dinner in Dad's office, when someone came through the door. When I looked, I caught the side of my head on the leg of the table. This caused an injury to my left eye. It was very painful and I didn't realise at the time the damage I had caused. When I went to see Mum in the evening, she said, "Jenny, what on earth have you done? Your eye is all red and swollen." I jumped on to Mum's bed to get a bit of fuss and let Mum have a closer look at the damage. Mum gave my eye a close inspection. I whimpered a little when she touched around the area. Dad explained what had happened. "You will have to take Jenny to the vet, I don't think she can see properly out of that eye. I am not sure whether it will be permanent or not."

Oh no, not the vet man again, I thought. I'm not too keen on that! Mum put a cover over my good eye. This is silly, Mum, it's the other eye that's poorly, I thought. When Mum took the cover off my good eye, she told Dad that I couldn't see at all out of my bad eye. I wondered how Mum knew that. After all, she couldn't see what I was seeing (or not seeing, as the case may be). Dad took me to the vet man the next day. He said I would never see out of that eye ever again.

I wasn't too worried about only having one eye, because I was getting used to it now. Anyway, I knew Mum would sort things out to help me, like she did when I started to go deaf. When Dad told Mum what the vet man said, she was very upset to start with. She didn't like it when I was in pain or hurt in any way. I think it was because she had a lot of pain herself and knew what it felt like. Mum sat and stroked me. She said she would rather have my pain than see me hurting. That's typical of Mum.

The following day, in the afternoon, Mum got on the floor with me. "Now, Jenny," she said, "we are going to have to learn how to cope with you being blind in one eye, as well as being deaf. Don't worry, we will sort it out." I wasn't worried at all, I knew Mum would work something out. After all; she did before, didn't she?

Mum told me to sit at the side of her, then she put my ball in front of my good eye. "Look, Jenny, and watch," she said. I did as I was told and looked at the ball. Mum threw the ball and then pointed in the direction the ball went. I ran and got the ball and gave it back to Mum. Over and over again, Mum threw the ball and followed the direction it took with her finger. All of a sudden, I realised what Mum was doing, because the last time Mum did it, she didn't follow the direction with her finger. I didn't know which way to go, because Mum threw it on my blind side. I stood still, waited, and looked at Mum for directions. "Good girl, Jenny. Yes, you've got the idea. You look at me any time you are not too sure of where I want to go, or if you didn't hear me, and I will point it out to you." To make sure I really understood, Mum sat in her chair and told me to sit on the settee. Then Mum called "Jenny", while clapping her hands. When I looked at her she drew through the air with her finger where she wanted me to go. I followed her instructions and went straight to the right side of her wheelchair and sat down. "Very good. Who's a clever girl?" she said and gave me some fuss. I squeaked and jumped around in delight. Mum's a clever girl, that's who, not me! I knew Mum would work things out for me, so I wasn't worried about being deaf or blind in one eye.

Mum didn't stop there either. We worked as one, watching each other all the time. Mum looked out for me and I looked to her for instruction. One day I bumped into Dad's chair because it was on my blind side and I didn't hear Mum's instructions. This worried Mum. She said, "Oh Jenny, we must have another signal I can give you so you don't hurt yourself. We will work it out this afternoon."

During the afternoon, Mum came up with a good idea, after a few trials. That is, Mum sat in front of me on the floor and said in a loud and clear voice, "Jenny, stop!" As she said it, she put her hand up in front of my good eye. I sat still and didn't move. Mum then had a little play with me in our new way, then suddenly said, "Jenny, stop!" and put her hand up in front of my good eye. I stood still and didn't move an inch. I understood straight away what she was doing. "Well done, very good, you are very clever. Who said you can't teach an old dog new tricks!" I didn't understand the last bit, but Mum was very pleased and so was I.

Mum's emergency stop came into use sooner than either of us thought it would. A couple of days later, I was coming into the kitchen from the garden and was on my way to the lounge when all of a sudden, I heard "Jenny, stop!" and Mum's hand came in front of my good eye. I stopped in my tracks and didn't move an inch. Mum came over to me and drew with her finger in the air so I followed the way Mum showed me. After I was around the danger, Mum showed me that I would have bumped into the leg of the kitchen table. I could have bumped my head on that table, damaged my good eye and be blind in both, if it hadn't been for Mum. You know how you people who can't see have guide dogs to help them? The dog sees for its owner and guides them so they don't hurt themselves. Well, in this case, I have a guide person for the blind dog!

We were both what people would call "disabled", but to us life was good in every way and we were happy and that's all that mattered. To me and Mum our problems didn't matter. We just carried on living our lives in our adapted way; we had no problem we couldn't sort out.

CHAPTER NINETEEN

YOU KNOW HOW THE BACK DOOR IS OPEN ALL day in the summer and I can run in and out whenever I want to? Well, sometimes I wish Mum could come outside and play with me instead of just sitting in the doorway watching. I think – well, I know – Mum would have done anything to get out in the fresh air. At times I would feel guilty that Mum couldn't come outside, while I could run up and down our garden whenever I wanted to. Mum never said anything about it. She was just pleased that I had that freedom.

One day, as Mum sat in the doorway, she looked sad. I went up to her to give her some fuss. Mum gave me a pat and a kiss on my nose and said, "Jenny, I really want to be out there with you so much it hurts." I did what I could to comfort her. I wished I could carry her outside. I would have done if I could, but I'm not a big dog.

It was now cup-of-tea time and we went into the lounge. After our tea, Mum lay on the settee so I gently climbed onto her chest and put my face next to hers and kissed her. Mum cried. She was holding me tight and her tears wet my fur. I just kissed and comforted Mum for a while, letting her know I understood how she felt. I know how I felt when I couldn't go in the garden when the weather was cold in the winter time. After a while, Mum said, "It's all right now, Jenny. I've got over it again for a while, so let's have a playtime; and make ourselves happy again before Dad gets home from work."

I made it a special playtime; I let Mum have the ball more than usual. By the time we were finished, Mum was back to her usual self again. "I think I will have to talk to your Dad and see if we can have a small patio built, so I can at least get outside the door," Mum said. I didn't know what a patio was, but if it would get Mum outside, then I was all for it.

Mum must have talked to Dad about it because a couple of weeks later, a man came and looked at the garden. He measured how big the patio thing could be. After talking to Mum about it, the man left. Mum called me, "Jenny, come and sit on Mummy's lap." Once on Mum's lap, she took us to the back door in her chair. We sat looking out into the garden and Mum said, "If it's not too expensive, I will be able to go outside in a few weeks' time." Then she went on to explain what a patio was and how big it would be. Mum had a big smile on her face as she spoke. Mum would only be able to go on the top end of the garden, but she didn't mind, because at least she would get outside with me.

The weather was getting cold now. It had been several weeks since Mum spoke to that man. I wondered when it was all going to happen. Then one day, Mum seemed very excited. This must be the day the man's coming, I thought. Sure enough, it wasn't long before a big van pulled up outside our house. I ran to tell Mum. We both were excited now. The back gate was opened and things were brought into the garden. I sat and watched the men work through the window in the back door. After a while, I needed to do a wee-wee, but how do I get into the garden with all that mess there? I went up to Mum and told her I needed to go out. Mum went to open the back door, then realised that I couldn't get over all the mess. She asked the man if he would take me out the front door and around to the garden through the back gate. He was very kind and duly obliged. I did my wee-wee (which was difficult because I didn't like the men being able to see me do it). Mum realised and told the men not to look in my direction, then I would be all right. Afterwards, the man took me back around to the front door and into the lounge. This was all right and we did it that way every time I needed to go out.

The men worked very hard for nearly a week. The patio was looking very good. I was pleased when all the mess was cleared away though, so I could go out the back door again. The men did the finishing bits and pieces. Mum said they would bring tubs to put along the front so she wouldn't fall over the edge into the garden. I could jump down, but it was far too high for Mum's chair to get down.

It was late afternoon and Dad came home from work just as the men were packing away. They put a piece of wood the kitchen side of the door and another piece from the door over to the patio, because of the little step. I ran outside with Dad and the garden man. Mum lined up her chair and went up and over both ramps and landed outside. As Mum got onto the patio, she screamed out loud with excitement. It was wonderful to see her so happy. I went jumping around Mum, squeaking with happiness to show her I joined her in her excitement. Dad and the garden man laughed. They talked for a while about tubs to make it safer, then the garden man left. Mum just sat there, looking and smiling. Dad went back into the house, saying he was cold. He kept coming out to Mum saying, "Are you coming in now? It's cold and dark. Anyway it's only a patio." He went back inside. I sat at Mum's side; I understood it meant more to Mum than just being a patio – it was a bit of freedom. Mum tapped her lap, so I jumped up and sat looking down the garden. "Can you smell that fresh air, Jenny? It's so wonderful. I will be able to sit out here with you in the warmer weather, or even in the rain." I turned and gave her a kiss to show her I understood. Mum has a thing about being in the rain. When I was younger, and Mum could walk, we would often go for walks in the rain. It was nice, and when we got home, Mum would always dry me before she dried herself. My fur would go fluffy and Mum said it had a nice fresh smell.

Dad eventually persuaded Mum to go back into the house. The tubs came the following day; they were big and very heavy. The needed to be like that, so Mum could pull herself up or lean on them. Mum put some plants and what she called bulbs in the tubs. "In a few weeks' time the tubs will be full of flowers, Jenny. It will look very pretty." Mum was right; those tubs were full of colour, but it seemed to take a lot longer than a few weeks.

The better weather finally arrived. Mum had been growing things called "seeds" in a tray. These seeds didn't look very big, so she would need a lot of them to fill the tubs. The seeds were mainly brown in colour when Mum planted them, but she said they would grow and become green. I would go to the back bedroom with Mum every day to watch. She would spray them with water and then turn the trays. All I could see to start with was the brown soil, but as time went on, little green things appeared. The green things got bigger and bigger, as Mum sprayed them. Mum did something I didn't really understand. She took these, now little things called plants, out of those trays and put them into other trays. This time, the plants were further apart – something to do with giving roots more room.

One sunny day, Mum took all the colourful flowers out of the tubs. She said it was now time to put the new plants out. I sat and watched while Mum did all the work. Well, I couldn't help because I didn't know what to do. I must say, it didn't look that colourful when she had finished. They didn't smell of much either. Then one day, I noticed bits of colour showing, more and more colours came out each day. Mum called to me when she was sitting outside one day, "Jenny, see I told you the plants would have flowers. In another couple of weeks, these tubs will be overflowing with colours and smells." I sniffed one, just to be sure and they did smell. And all this came from those little brown seeds – it's amazing really!

We had a lovely summer (that's what the hot days are called), with Mum popping outside whenever she wanted to. I enjoyed sitting with her. Sometimes I would sit on her lap and we would talk for a while. Not that there was much room for us with all those tubs overflowing everywhere. I am glad we got that patio – it gave both me and Mum a lot of pleasure.

Dad came out sometimes, just to have a look. He didn't look after the plants like Mum did. The trouble is, the sunny days changed back into the cold days and once Mum had changed the flowers again, she stayed in the house. Can't wait for the sunny days to come back, so we can sit outside together again.

CHAPTER TWENTY

TIME HAS PASSED. I AM NOW GETTING ON IN years – well, that's what Mum calls it. Mum and Dad are older too, but I don't know how old they are because they never tell me. Mum is always telling people I am sixteen years old in people years, and then she says I am a hundred and twelve years old in doggy years. I don't know what she means, but I wish she would make up her mind! It doesn't matter to me how old I am because it doesn't really mean anything. I think you are as old as you feel and I don't feel any older, but I think my body does.

In the mornings now, I feel a little bit stiff when I first start to move. Sometimes, as well, through the day I find it difficult to jump up onto the settee. I was taken to see the vet man to get something called tablets because Mum said I had someone called "Arthur Eye-Tuss". I don't think I have met him before. Well, that's what I think she called it, and Mum should know; she has it herself. See, I told you we share everything! Mum put the tablet thing in my food. She did try to make me swallow it, but I spat it out. Well, she tried several times to be honest, but it didn't taste very nice, so I wouldn't swallow it. It must have helped me, because my legs didn't hurt so much.

After taking these tablets for a few days, Mum said I must do some exercises to keep my joints moving.

Now I did understand a little about it because Mum has done exercises before.

One afternoon, Mum called to me, "Jenny, come and lie on the floor. I want to move your legs!"

Move my legs! I move my legs all the time, if I didn't I wouldn't be able to walk, would I? What is Mum on about now? Mind you, Mum being Mum must have her reasons; she has done in the past, hasn't she? I went over to Mum and lay on the floor as she asked. Mum got out of her chair and crawled across to me. First of all, she felt all the way up each leg, starting from the paw. Then she bent and straightened each leg to its full movement. It was a little painful when she first did it. Mind you, by the time Mum had finished, I felt so relaxed I nearly fell asleep.

After a few minutes, Mum said, "Come on Jenny, wake up, we will have a playtime now." I didn't move. I was enjoying it so much, I just wanted Mum to carry on. "Wakey-wakey, Jenny, you crafty little thing. You have to run about now, but we will do it again tomorrow." I slowly got up and had a stretch and yawned. Mum suddenly shouted "*Boo!*" It made me jump, but it woke me up. We started to play with my ball, then we had a chase game. We played for quite a while. Mum said, "That's blown all the cobwebs away and got our heartbeats racing; now I'll put the kettle on and we will have a cup of tea." Well, Mum might have blown cobwebs away, but I didn't, because I didn't see any, but I wasn't looking really, I just played. I was ready for cup-of-tea time, though.

I think there is more to this playtime than Mum lets on. When we used to play, we just played. I would run around wherever I wanted to go. Now, if I went the same way too many times, Mum would throw my ball to make me turn the other way. "Come on Jenny, use the other two legs more. I know it hurts, but it will make them stronger," Mum would say. Mum always got me to do things I didn't want to do by making it fun.

I remember one day, my legs hurt a lot and I didn't feel very well. Mum realised I wasn't well, so she just moved my legs without the playtime. I was allowed a couple of days without running around playtime, and then Mum said I must move about or my legs will get stiff. I wasn't too keen; I slowly got onto the floor and lay down again. Mum was crafty; she put chocolate buttons on the floor right across the room. I managed to get the first one by stretching my neck out as far as I could. I ate it quickly and tried to get the next one, but it was just out of my reach. I looked at Mum as if to ask her to put it closer so I didn't have to get up. Mum said, "No, Jenny, come on, you have to stand up and walk to get it. I'm not giving it to you." She tapped the floor to encourage me, her voice was soft and gentle. "Come and get it, there's a good girl. Do it for Mummy." Well, how could I refuse after that? I slowly pushed myself up and walked over to the next chocolate button and claimed my reward. Mum moved to the next button and encouraged me again. This went on until all the buttons were eaten. I must admit, once I got moving, it did get easier. After that, I was allowed to go back on the settee and have a nap.

I started to find it difficult to get onto the bed at night. I would manage to get up the stairs, but the bed was a lot higher than that. I would put my front paws onto the bed then wait for Mum to crawl up to me, so she could give me a helping hand. I would look at Mum and then look down at my back legs indicating I was ready to be helped. I pulled myself up with my front legs at the same time Mum was lifting the back ones. This way we only had to lift half of my weight each. Mum wasn't strong enough to lift all of me. Not that I was overweight, but Mum's arms and legs hurt like mine. Sometimes Dad would lift my bottom half onto the bed, but he is strong and doesn't know Arthur Eye-Tuss. Sometimes, when I was at the bottom of the stairs thinking abut the climb ahead, Dad would scoop me up into his arms, take me up and put me straight on to the bed. I think Mum wished he could do the same for her sometimes.

I needed help in the same way to get on to the settee at times. Mum always made me have a go before she would help me, which is not a bad thing. All I had to do after trying was look at Mum and then look at my rear end. Mum would then get on to the floor and together we would give a push until I was on the settee. I always felt sorry that I had to make Mum get onto the floor, but she didn't mind. Mum said I looked after her, so now she will look after me. As far as I am concerned, Mum has looked after me ever since that first night all that time ago.

CHAPTER TWENTY-ONE

WELL, THIS HAS BEEN MY LIFE. IT HAS BEEN A long and very happy life living here with Mum and Dad. We have shared a lot of ups and downs since that first evening when I was taken away from my sisters. Do you remember I wondered if the lady would be nice and give me a lot of love? Well, I have had so much love given to me from my mum and dad, words just can't say. The way Mum and I knew how each of us felt at any time of the day and night was wonderful; we were as one.

There is so much more I could tell you about my life, but it is special for just me and Mum. I loved the summers when we would go out for a ride in the car. Mum would always pack something called a picnic, so we could sit on a blanket on the grass in the sunshine. As soon as we got on the blanket, Mum would give me a drink; she always packed my dish. I always got my drink before Dad, but he didn't mind. There was a square thing Mum would take out of the picnic box that was very cold. Mum would put it under the blanket where I lay and it cooled me down when the sun was too hot. We always sat under a tree or something, so it was in the shade. Mum always thought of everything it seemed.

At these picnics I had different food from when we were at home. Mum called some of it chicken, and I liked chicken a lot, but there were all different bits and pieces too. Sometimes after eating, Dad would get Mum's chair out of the car and we would go for a little walk. I liked these picnics and so did Mum, and we made the most of being outside in the fresh air.

Special times like Christmas day I enjoyed too. Mum and Dad would open lots of coloured packages and have new things. Mum would also have something new for me too. At dinner time, I had a special dinner which was like chicken and a sausage thing with vegetables. I always ate my chicken bits first, but I liked the orange vegetable too. Mum gave me green things one year, but it upset my tummy! I didn't have that ever again.

I say these were special times, but with Mum, every day was special. The only times I didn't like were the times when Mum had to go away into those hospital places. Mind you, when Mum got home after being there, we both made up for it. Yes, I can say that I have been very lucky living with my mum and dad. Mum would show me pictures and read me things about other animals that didn't have a nice home. Some of these animals looked thin and had been hurt in some way. It made me shiver to see it. It upset my mum; she sends money to a place that helps animals that have been hurt. I think, if she could, she would have them all and give them love like she gives me.

I think I have been very lucky when I look back over my life. I have had a nice home and garden to run and play in. All I ever needed has been provided, like food and healthcare and more, much more, in the love that has poured out from Mum and Dad to me. As I think back to the days in the kennel with my sisters, I can only hope that they have been as happy as I have. Thank you, Mum and Dad!

CPSIA information can be obtained at www.ICGtesting.com
Printed in the USA
LVOW11s0724030516

486318LV00001B/22/P